Gardening from Scratch

Xenia Field

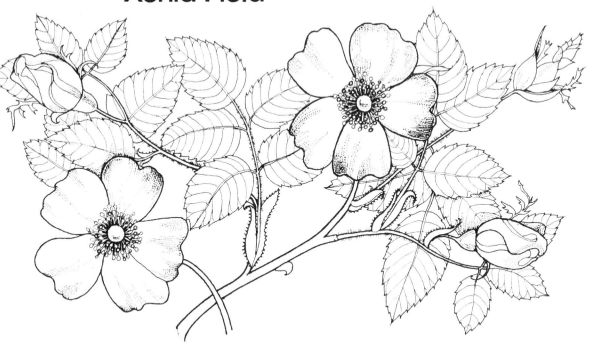

HAMLYN
London · New York · Sydney · Toronto

Acknowledgements
Line drawings by Patricia Clements
Colour photographs by Harry Smith

First published in 1973 by
THE HAMLYN PUBLISHING GROUP LIMITED
LONDON · NEW YORK · SYDNEY · TORONTO
Astronaut House, Feltham, Middlesex, England
Printed in England by Cox & Wyman Limited,
Fakenham, Norfolk
Filmset in England by V. Siviter Smith and
Company Limited, Birmingham
Second impression, 1974

ISBN 0 600 33842 8

Contents

Foreword

This is a book for the beginner. It is hoped it will pave the way to the more difficult text book, often a headache to the gardener starting from scratch.

I offer basic information, hoping to guide the learner step by step and avoid the temptation of telling him too much too quickly.

The book is for the gardener who inherits, not an estate, but a small garden, strip or patch. This garden may look remarkably unattractive if the builder has only lately gone out of the gate leaving the usual ugly debris behind him. Or it may consist of a small, overgrown wilderness with border and beds choked with weeds. Few of us have the luck to take over a garden in good order and there is, as a rule, much hard work waiting to be done.

But this garden, beyond all others, has something very endearing about it. It is yours to care for.

You will find the work the purest of pleasures. Once you have a garden of your own the matter is settled for all time; you will be a gardener, with or without a garden, forever and forever.

Let me help you dig your way, at a reasonable pace, into your garden.

Xenia Field

Part I
The Practicalities of Gardening

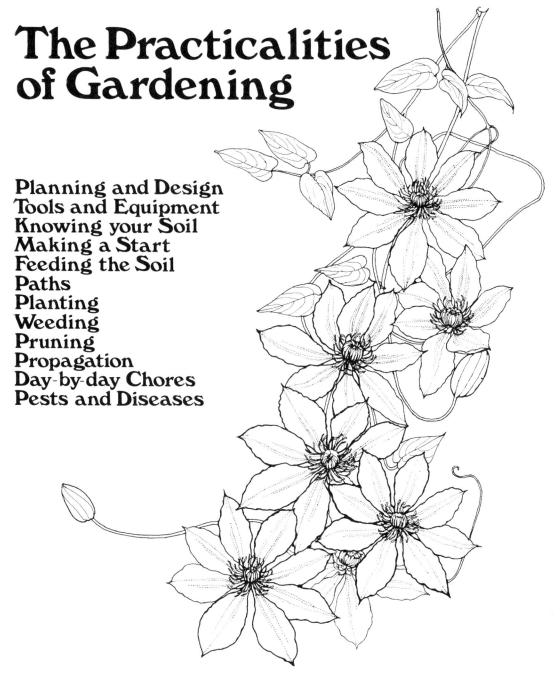

Planning and Design
Tools and Equipment
Knowing your Soil
Making a Start
Feeding the Soil
Paths
Planting
Weeding
Pruning
Propagation
Day-by-day Chores
Pests and Diseases

Planning and Design

Every garden should be individual, so I offer no formula, but would point out that to be successful a garden should have a design either on paper or in the mind. A general pattern before you start will save much slavery later on.

The best designs are simple and balanced and the lines of beds and borders generous rather than fussy and irritating. The spacing, sequence of colour and perspective are even more important in a small garden than in the rolling land of Windsor or Chatsworth. A well-placed shrub, tree, statue or ornament can be used as a focal point to break any monotony or straight lines but too many distractions are a mistake.

Colour is usually demanded by the town gardener. Those with heavily shaded gardens will have to work a little harder than the rest to maintain interest and should pay extra attention to texture and form. Silver foliage plants like the friendly Lamb's Ear with its grey nap foliage will be found a blessing.

Visiting other people's gardens is helpful in stimulating the imagination and a large garden, on occasion, is not too grand to supply an idea to the owner of a pocket-handkerchief plot. There should be no fear of imitation, so long as the gardener holds on to his own ideas. There are a thousand ways of making a garden – informal, symmetrical, stylised, or frankly artificial with the aid of mirrors and other gadgets.

The expense of making the garden and keeping it up will influence the design, and there may be domestic items such as the children's sandpit, and anything from the washing line to the dustbin to be concealed. Above all privacy must be maintained and treasured.

Illusion with an element of surprise is exciting. The unexpected planting that presents itself round a corner or shrubbery is especially attractive but these features are easier to arrange in the large rather than the small garden. Fortunately, there are no rules and I enjoy fruit trees on the lawn and artichokes, rhubarb and fringed white, pink, and purple variegated cabbage (kale) in the border.

There are, however, two indispensable items for me: a pleasing view from the windows and somewhere to sit, a paved, sheltered spot close to the house where it is pleasant to work or dream.

How can a well-designed garden be best described? As a garden where, when the summer flowers and autumn foliage no longer decorate the scene, the basic design remains intact.

Tools and Equipment

Good tools help to make a good gardener, and without them he cannot give of his best. Only lately I came across a frustrated beginner, his brow dripping with sweat, digging with a deplorable-looking shovel. There are dozens of gardeners battling with rusty, blunt implements and spades which are far too heavy.

Gardening tools should be of high quality and bear the name of an established firm. If the manufacturer has a reputation worth keeping the gardener is likely to be in safe hands. Economise if you will in the number of your tools but never buy cheap ones. Weak tools, the rake and hoe heads which are poorly fastened so that they first waggle and then fall off, are all too common. It pays to buy tools of as good a quality as the budget will allow.

Gardening Clothes

It is of little importance what you wear so long as your clothes allow you to bend and stretch and keep you dry. Woolly clothes are a menace when pruning roses. Tough denims or other close-weave material is the best protection against thorns.

Boots are better than shoes for hard work and heavy soil and you'll find a stout pair of boots a blessing. If you scrape, brush and treat them with dubbin after wearing they will soften up like doeskin. Clay is most easily removed by being washed off.

Good, easy-to-use pockets come in handy. Trousers with turn-ups are to be avoided. Whenever possible clothing should be cheerful: there is no necessity to wear the uniform of the scarecrow.

Spade

There are four basic tools of which the spade is the kingpin. It is important to choose one of the right length and weight, to match your strength. The length of the spade and the size of the blade will determine the weight that can be lifted.

Young gardeners, like young golfers, are tempted to buy tools which they have not the physical power to handle with the desired rhythm.

If there is any possibility of a full-sized spade tiring you buy a lighter one. For women, other than Amazons, a boy's

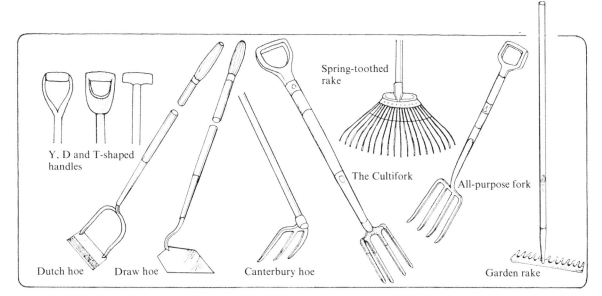

Y, D and T-shaped handles

Dutch hoe Draw hoe Canterbury hoe

Spring-toothed rake

The Cultifork All-purpose fork

Garden rake

spade is often the best weight. I find that the D- or Y-shaped rather than the T-shaped handle raises fewer blisters, but opinions are divided on this so try all three and choose the grip that suits you best. Smooth ash or plastic handles and, if the budget will run to it, stainless steel blades are the ideal.

The treaded spade with a ridge on the top of the upper side will reduce wear on shoes, but in spite of this the majority of gardeners prefer a spade without the tread.

Fork

You will require an all-purpose fork for spreading manure, lifting plants and potatoes, and general spring and summer forking. There are special models for heavy and light soils, border digging and potato lifting. The gardener should go for a medium fork with four prongs.

May I suggest your trying the Cultifork, designed by me for the gardener with a crowded border who finds bending with a hand fork difficult. This fork, made by Spear and Jackson, has four straight prongs: it is curved like a sugar scoop, is light and remarkably helpful in carrying out all the familiar tasks of the square fork.

The Cultifork has been welcomed by well-known horticulturists and I think you will like it.

Pronged Cultivator

This implement with its three curved prongs breaks up the soil, leaving a nice growing tilth. It is excellent for the weaker gardener when tackling largish areas of rough, unplanted ground. If gardening on a small scale it is better to borrow as it is scarcely worth buying one. Once the ground is nicely broken up the rest of the work can be done with hoe and rake.

Hoe

There are numerous hoes for scarifying (breaking up the surface), loosening the weeds and aerating the hard crust of the soil, so that the plants can breathe. These include the Dutch hoe, the draw hoe, the triangular hoe and the Canterbury hoe.

The Dutch hoe, with a D-shaped blade and a head firmly fixed on to a 5-ft. handle, is my pick for the novice. A small hand hoe is also a help when hoeing along seed rows and in tight corners.

The draw hoe is useful for making seed drills, and the gardener on clay will find the short-handled draw hoe a grand implement for breaking up clods.

Rake

There are rakes and rakes but it is best to start off with a handy light 12-in. steel rake which is properly shafted, even if it is a little more expensive than its brothers. It will teach you to rake and enjoy it. Avoid the pressed sheet metal rake and other deceivers. A spring-toothed rake is excellent for scarifying and cleaning out debris from turf.

Trowel

The scoop-shaped trowel is one of the most important small tools for weeding and planting and is available in stainless steel with a short, easy-grip handle, preferably of ash.

Hand Fork

This useful weeding tool should possess a short handle and three flat prongs. The pressed steel and the hollow-handled type should be avoided.

Dibber

The blunt and snub-nosed dibber for planting seedlings can be bought or made at home. The sharp-pointed dibber is a danger, since it often leaves an air pocket beneath the unfortunate seedling.

Knife

A pocket knife is useful for cutting twine and dead heading. The blade must be of good quality and of medium size. To be effective, it must be kept really sharp; the gardener who learns to use a whetstone for this purpose comes off best.

Secateurs
Pruners must be of a reputable make. They will last far longer if oiled occasionally.

Watering Can
Whether a galvanised metal or plastic can is chosen, it should be well balanced and include a rose fitting for the spout. The can should always be emptied and stood on its head when not in use. A second watering can, dabbed with red paint as a warning, should be kept for weedkillers and other substances toxic to plant life, and used for nothing else.

Shears
These should be notched for dealing with the tougher stems when cutting hedges, possess a good thick pivot and strong cutting power, and have well-spaced handles. They should not be too heavy or they will prove tiring to use.

Long-handled edging shears are invaluable for keeping the lawn trimmed.

Measuring Rod
A ruler is particularly useful when making a new garden and can be made at home from a straight piece of seasoned timber marked off in convenient lengths.

Hose Pipe
A hose is invaluable for saving time and energy when watering, and if rolled on a reel so much the better. The cheaper plastic hose is worth consideration, being less likely to perish than rubber.

Sprayer
A sprayer will be needed for spraying roses and other plants that attract pests. Many types of pressure sprayer are available in plastic, the choice of size depending on the area to be covered. The sprayer should be rinsed through with clear water immediately after being used.

Two types of sprayer: a hand sprayer with trigger action and a knapsack pressure sprayer

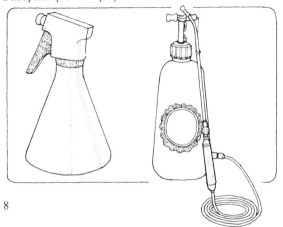

Fertiliser Distributor for Lawns
This aid can be obtained from a garden centre and proves, as a rule, an economy. Spreading fertiliser by hand is particularly difficult in a wind and only too often the beginner scorches the grass's top growth by uneven distribution. The distributor can also be used for sowing seed evenly over a large area, such as a new lawn. Small areas can be hand sown and even distribution ensured by mixing the seed with sand.

Wheelbarrow
The oak or elm barrow fitted with cushion-tyre wheel is long lasting if kept under cover but the newer types of barrow in lightweight galvanised steel are easier to balance and manoeuvre over soft ground and they cause less strain on the arms.

Roller
A heavy roller is liable to compact the soil and can be a menace in the hands of a novice. The roller on a cylinder-type mower is quite adequate for firming up the lawn.

Mower
Many types of mower are available in a wide range of prices. From among these there are two cutting principles to choose from: the reel or revolving cylinder type with three or more cutting blades, or the rotary mower with a single rotating cutting blade. The reel mower with wheels at the sides which drive the cutting blades is the simplest and lightest to use of the hand-propelled machines, though it will not cut the edges of the lawn. The cutting blades of a cylinder mower are operated by a lightweight roller or cylinder at the back of the machine and this enables it to be taken right up to the edge of the grass. Both give a close cut and fine finish to the lawn, creating the striped effect so much admired by some gardeners. The rotary-type mower, though less precise, is perhaps more flexible as it will tackle long or damp grass and is not so likely to jam on uneven tufts.

Mowers may be hand propelled or powered by a battery, mains electric or petrol-driven motor, the choice depending on individual requirements. (See Lawns, p. 29.)

Care of Tools
Allow yourself five minutes' grace when knocking off work to clean your tools before putting them away. First scrape or wash the clay from all and sundry, then rub over with sacking or rough material, afterwards finishing off with a wipe from an oily rag.

Warning
Any form of mechanical cutter must be used with respect. Boots or sturdy shoes save accidents. Sandals or canvas shoes are a menace. And above all, keep sharp implements out of the way of children and animals.

If a machine should jam, power must be switched off before any attempt is made to set the blades free.

Knowing your Soil

Soil plays a vital part in gardening. Unfortunately it often sounds a deadly dull subject and in many a well-thumbed text book the pages on soil remain clean, and unread.

I came across a library copy of such a book in which a reader had pencilled a significant note. 'I am not a chemist, scientist nor horticulturist. One would need to be all three to understand you, drat you!'

When you stop thinking of your soil as a slab of dirt and look upon it as a living thing you have taken a first step in the right direction. The successful gardener has a picture in mind of his soil eating, drinking and breathing and requiring food, drink and air.

Now, whether you are the tenant of a garden which has been cultivated or the owner of a virgin strip, the first thing you must do is to find out something about the soil. What have the millions of years done for your piece of ocean floor or land? What has happened to the primeval rocks? What have the floods and earthquakes (and the modern builder) left behind?

How to Find Out

There are obvious pointers. If the soil sticks to your boots and feels clammy and soapy between finger and thumb, then it is likely to be clay. If in reasonably fine weather the the soil trickles through your fingers as fast as money then the clay is well bolstered with sand – perhaps too much.

The varied wild flowers and weeds that the land invites will also give some of the answers. 'When I see nettles and them buttercups I feel the damp in my bones,' a farmer told me. Chicory will be found on chalky or light soil, groundsel on loam, quaking grass on poor, hungry land, and the lovely cowslip on the clay that it dotes upon. But if you do not yet recognise the wild flowers and weeds when you see them you are not much better off than before. The man who cannot spell at all may find a dictionary an added embarrassment.

Trees and shrubs also have a tale to tell. Firs and larches will be found on poor soil where the oak, demanding better fare, will not deign to grow. Birches and willow seek the damp marshland; beech will search for lime, while the rose clings to the heavier clay; the rhododendrons, azaleas and heath revel in peat and, as Reginald Arkell wrote: 'A rhododendron grown on lime looks like a clergyman doing time.'

If the oak and ash trees around you are fine and handsome, the hedges dense with growth and the meadows a rich green you may take it as an accepted sign that the soil is good and that you'll be able to grow most things. If the trees are dwarfed and you can peer through the thin hedges you'll have to work hard to make things grow.

There are handy outfits obtainable at the chemist's, garden centre or nursery for a few shillings which enable the gardener to make a rough test for acidity. When brought into contact with the soil the small colour indicator will turn pink if the soil is peat and acid, and blue when lime and alkaline. Acidity and alkalinity are measured by the pH scale; pH7 stands for neutral, anything below being acid, anything above alkaline. Home testing is a useful experience provided you bear in mind that different parts of the garden may give different results, but you can go one better than this by asking the gardener on the spot.

The Native Gardener

Professional or amateur, a gardener familiar with local conditions can be immensely helpful. He shouldn't be difficult to find on a fine Saturday afternoon; he'll be no further away than the next street or down the next lane. Make it clear to him at once that you are a newcomer and a beginner. Keep the question clear and short for he'll want to be getting on with the job. Ask him about the soil. Of course, it is possible for it to vary from foot to foot and a plant that will flower wonderfully on one side of the path has been known to turn up its toes on the other. There are scarcely two soils exactly alike but the answer you get from the man on the spot is well worth having.

Loam

If it is good loam you are in luck for there's nothing to beat it. It has a clay content which holds the moisture and a nice amount of sand which provides a pleasant, easy root-run for almost any plant.

Loam soil never suffers from quick drying out, yawning cracks in the summer drought, or waterlogging. There are no swamps following the winter rains. Meanwhile the plants have everything they can wish for: sand for ventilation, clay for moisture and a fair supply of humus-forming material. Good loam is gardener's luck and one may well wonder what one has done to deserve it.

Sandy Soil

Gritty to the touch, sandy soil is often described as hot and hungry. The trouble is that the rain rushes through it carrying off valuable nutrients; then, after the winter deluge the soil dries up like a desert and shrinks, resulting in air spaces that deprive roots of food and anchorage causing the plants to die of thirst.

The gardener must do all in his power to make the sand more retentive of moisture by digging in plenty of humus-forming material in the form of well-rotted animal manure, vegetable refuse, peat or treated sewage. These should be dug in during the winter. Dressings of bonemeal or organic fertilisers are also helpful. Bonemeal is slow acting and can be applied in winter, but most organic fertilisers are less likely to be washed out of the soil if applied in the spring when plants can make use of them. A top covering of lawn clippings (see Mulching, p. 24) or spent hops will help prevent summer baking.

Deep digging or trenching are not advised on this type of soil as they merely increase the pace of drainage.

Sandy soil is not, perhaps, desirable, but it is light to work and easily built up and improved. It has the advantage of warming up quickly and is capable of growing the tasty early vegetables and first flowers of the season, which are so much more glamorous than the rest.

Clay Soil

This type of soil is wet and always difficult and, let me say it for you, the very devil in winter. The mistake that most beginners make is to try to handle the stuff when it is sticky. This simply encourages the clay to pack down in lumps, driving out the air.

Digging should be done after a long spell of fine, dry days. If you dig and drain and work like a horse you will find you have some of the finest land in the world. The novice is apt to despair over the putty-like, gluey mass which turns into sunbaked clods in summer and cast-iron concrete when winter comes. But if he can succeed in breaking down the clay by digging it over in autumn to expose the larger lumps to weather action and frost, and by mixing it with plenty of rotted organic matter, this soil becomes rich and splendid and plants will love it.

It isn't the amount of humus-forming material, but the timing of its application and the competent way it is mixed with the clay that counts.

The addition of lime also helps to break down a heavy clay soil, by causing the minute clay particles to cling together and form larger granules which give the soil a more open texture. This process is known as 'flocculation'. But adding lime to the soil increases its alkalinity, so it is important to bear in mind the kind of plants to be grown – some, such as rhododendrons and heathers, are lime haters – and to test for acid/alkaline reaction.

There are also other chemical soil conditioners which improve the texture of heavy soils, though they do not contribute directly to their humus or plant food content. These undoubtedly help the gardener to solve the clay problem but they are an expensive alternative to his own labour, particularly in a large garden.

The gardener must be content to improve the condition of his beds one by one. Please do not think me unsympathetic, and let me assure you I realise there will be days when clay is unworkable. I never forget the old story of the gardener who committed suicide leaving but one word of explanation behind him: 'Clay.'

Chalk Soil

These must be fed as they are thin, hungry soils, often overlying limestone. However, chalk is quite popular with plants other than the lime haters such as rhododendrons, azaleas and lupins.

The gardener must increase the quantity of plant foods by working manure or compost into the top spit (see p. 11) or by mulching (see p. 24).

Chalk soil dries out quickly during a drought and plant foliage may turn yellow, warning the gardener that he must get busy with the hose and can, or better still, apply a mulch in late spring, once the soil has warmed up. This yellowing of foliage – a condition known as chlorosis – may also be due to lack of iron and magnesium, two elements essential to plants which become arrested by the excess calcium in a chalky soil. Heavy dressings of acid substances such as dung, peat and compost, help counteract the calcium and provide the humus needed.

Meanwhile a garden on newly broken chalk will benefit magically by dressings of potash and phosphates and epsom salts.

Every soil has its blessing. Chalk soil almost defeats club root disease which afflicts brassica crops.

Peat Soil

Peat is rich with fibrous vegetable matter and the product of decayed vegetation from bogs and marshes. Rhododendrons and azaleas revel in this acid soil and it is particularly enjoyed by celery.

Peat soil may prove a trifle sour (acid) for some plants such as pinks, and must be treated with lime in which it is usually lacking. I was brought up on a spongy, peaty soil and found that when kept in good heart and limed occasionally it would grow almost anything.

Summing Up

Here I end my brief classification of soil in the hope that a small part of the chapter will be read.

At a gardening brains trust I was asked what soil I should expect to find in heaven. I suggested $\frac{1}{6}$ part sand, $\frac{1}{6}$ sharp grit, $\frac{1}{4}$ clay, $\frac{1}{4}$ part humus and $\frac{1}{6}$ part chalk. Few of us get this on earth, but there is no harm in dreaming of heavenly loam.

Making a Start

Well, what sort of garden have you inherited? Has it been well cared for? Is it a garden to be proud of? Or just an overgrown jungle choked with weeds, tall grass and brambles – a garden so derelict that your heart slumps at the sight of it?

If the builder has failed to tidy up, leaving bricks, cement and debris in his tracks, I would advise calling him back to clear the site. The beginner should not be discouraged, for the neglected garden can be reclaimed more easily than it would at first appear, if he sets about it in the right way.

First, dead wood, unwanted undergrowth and long grass must be cut back so that the gardener can move around. Broken branches, unwanted and damaged trees and shrubs must be cut off and pulled up – or, in gardener's jargon, 'grubbed up'. The long grass is best scythed, provided the gardener is skilled in wielding the curved blade; otherwise he must resort to a sickle or a rotary grass cutter. The work undertaken will depend, to some extent, on what time of year you arrive on the scene. An overgrown herbaceous border should not be cut down during the summer, but left until the autumn or spring.

The debris, having been collected in one place, should be sorted and burnt or left to rot down. Now that the decks are sufficiently clear for digging the next job is to skim off any weeds with a sharp spade, taking only a suspicion of soil with them.

Digging

Let us go back again to the local veteran. Watch how well he digs, driving his spade vertically down into the earth right to its full length. He works at a steady pace and in perfect rhythm but he is not ashamed to stop every now and then and light his pipe.

Observe how the veteran's spade barely skims the soil. He spares his energy by never lifting the full spade higher than he need.

Single or Plain Digging

Large areas should be worked in strips, methodically row by row in straight lines.

A trench should be dug at the end of the plot about 15 in. wide and a spit deep (that is, the spade's depth, about 10 in.). The soil from the first trench should be moved to the opposite end of the plot where it can be used later for filling in the last trench. Then, working backwards, dig the next trench, throwing the soil forward into the first. Be sure you press your blade well down before lifting, making an incision at the side of each spadeful so that it comes away easily. Don't be over-ambitious: a slice of 5 to 6 in. is quite large enough to lift on heavy soil.

All roots and menacing-looking weeds should be picked up and put aside for burning.

Double Digging (Bastard Trenching)

First make a trench 10 in. deep and 2 ft. wide, stacking the outgoing soil at the opposite end of the plot as before. The soil at the bottom of the trench must now be forked until it is well broken up, and manure or compost worked in at the same time. A second trench is then opened directly behind the first and the topsoil from it thrown forward into the first trench. Manure should be worked into this topsoil as well. The soil in the second trench is then broken up with a fork, and the work is continued in the same way throughout the plot.

Here is the golden rule for the beginner: always keep the top spit at its right level. Normally, it is the best and most fertile soil and should therefore be placed where the plants can easily reach it. Never bury the top spit.

Hoeing

This chore is not as fashionable as it used to be and the theory that it conserves moisture by forming a mulch of loose soil and so reduces evaporation is arguable. However, hoeing remains vital if weeds are to be kept down and the gardener who hoes regularly throughout the summer rather than waits till the weeds appear has a chance of keeping them away altogether.

The Dutch hoe should be held at arm's length with the blade parallel to the surface of the soil. It is operated by a pushing motion, the cutting edge of the hoe breaking up the surface of the soil and destroying the weeds while the gardener walks slowly backwards. Once the soil is hoed, care should be taken not to tread on it again.

The draw hoe is used for weeding between crops and is operated with a chopping movement, the blade being drawn inwards in the reverse direction to the Dutch hoe, while the gardener moves slowly forward over the ground already worked. The beginner should watch the veteran cutting down the larger weeds with this tool, walking forward and working, as always, in rhythm. This hoe with its swan neck and broad shoulders is also useful for drawing soil up and round a plant or tree, for blanching celery, earthing up potatoes, mulching and for opening drills for seeds.

Raking

Here the gardener should relax and attempt long, smooth push and pull strokes, bring the unwanted stones, stubborn clods or debris towards him so that he can pick them up and dispose of them. A firm yet loose grip with muscles relaxed should be attempted while working both ways, up and down the plot and then across.

The novice is apt to think that raking is an easy game. It is only when he surveys the bumpy or even mountainous surface that he has created that he realises that there is quite a technique to it. Once again, he should watch the veteran treading the ground, breaking down the soil into a finer surface as he goes, before starting to rake, relying on skill that comes with years of experience.

The Gardener's 'Fine Tilth'

This is a favourite phrase that recurs in gardening books but its meaning is not always made clear.

The gardener's 'fine tilth' is a fine, crumbly soil, easily obtained on light land but requiring hard work on stubborn clay. Such a surface is essential before sowing seed in March and April whether in flower or vegetable garden or on the site for a new lawn. The smaller the seed the finer the tilth should be.

On a clay soil the breaking-down process must be started by digging in the autumn so that the frost, wind and rain can play their part. Large, well-shod feet are useful aids in breaking down some of the left-over clods when levelling the ground before raking. Any lumps that do not respond can be dealt a sharp blow with the back of a fork. Should the beginner make the mistake of sticking the tines into sticky clay he may have difficulty in getting them out again.

Tips

Never work the soil when it is wet. Never dig when the ground is frosty. Apart from the back-breaking labour, it is a grave mistake to bury frosty soil for it will take a long time to warm up.

The beginner should get to know the look and feel of fertile soil. He should make a ball or dumpling of it in his hand. When in 'good heart' as the gardener's phrase has it, this will crumble under its own weight, not cling nor stick to his fingers, while a pinch of it pressed between finger and thumb will smear, not crumble. Fertile soil is lovely stuff.

Feeding the Soil

The gardener is constantly told that he must feed the soil by adding humus.

Humus

What is humus? Broadly speaking, animal and vegetable matter which fungi and bacteria (microbes) break down into plant food. Humus holds the moisture, ventilates the soil and makes it easy for plant roots to travel.

Humus-forming materials include animal manures, compost, leafmould, seaweed, peat, spent hops, straw and animal residues such as shoddy, offal and fish waste. The presence of humus does not necessarily represent high food value; animal manure is highly nutritious to plants and peat scarcely at all, though both make good humus. What it does do is to improve the texture of the soil and, more important still, stimulates the bacteria to change the chemicals in the soil into a form that plants can use. This is why feeding the soil is the key to successful gardening. Decayed organic matter is the raw material, the microbes are the workers and the by-product, humus.

Horse and Farmyard Manure

This is a useful provider of humus and being fibrous is helpful not only in keeping heavy land open but also in providing the necessary body to light and sandy soils. Though not long lasting it is slow acting and particularly good for improving heavy clay.

Alas, horse manure is becoming very difficult to come by. However, one barrowful to 10 sq. yd. will help to make some of your dreams come true. I should remind enthusiasts, still to be seen in the road with searching eye and empty shovel, that fresh manure which is not rotted down is harmful. If put close to plant roots it will burn them.

Manure should either be dug into vacant ground during the autumn or stored in a heap, under cover if possible – if washed by rain its food value will be lost – and turned over frequently sides to centre.

Pig and Poultry Manure

These are stronger than horse manure and must be well rotted before use and applied sparingly. They are a helpful and more lasting addition to light soil or to the compost heap.

Poultry manure improves if allowed to dry to powder in a closed bin. It can then be scattered or applied at the rate of $1\frac{1}{2}$ lb. to the square yard, but direct contact with plants should be avoided.

Liquid Manure

This is made by hanging a small sack containing well-rotted animal droppings in a barrel of water. The beginner should be careful not to apply the liquid in too strong a form. The strength is judged by the colour and consistency of the liquid; weak tea or pale ale is the shade to go for.

Liquid manure is a drink for the mature and healthy; it is not suitable for young seedlings nor for plants which have recently been potted.

Compost

The compost heap is composed of kitchen and garden refuse such as grass clippings, soft hedge trimmings and vegetable leaves which, when thoroughly rotted down, is dug into the soil to provide a good source of humus. Compost is a useful alternative when manure is hard to come by, giving bulk as well as nutriment and improving the texture of the soil. More about that later in the section on the compost heap, p. 14.

Fertilisers

The three main ingredients required by plants are nitrogen, phosphorus and potash. A compound fertiliser is ready mixed and contains a balance of all three. Nitrogen encourages foliage growth whether it be of Busy Lizzie or cabbages. Phosphorus assists the development of roots and the ripening of certain fruits and seeds. Potash enhances colour and increases resistance to disease in plants and is a health tonic, much appreciated by peas, beans and soft fruits.

The fertiliser list is a long one but the problem of choice is simplified for the beginner who can buy a complete or general fertiliser, containing all three foods in one, which will suit the majority of plants. Later on when he has gained more knowledge and experience the needs of the individual plants can be studied.

Now a word about the groups under which fertilisers are sold.

The Organic

These are made from plant and animal residues such as hoof and horn (the tomato's favourite food), fish or blood manure, steamed bone flour, dried blood, which has a magical effect on growth when applied in spring, seaweed and bonemeal, a slow-acting winter feed appreciated by one and all. Soot from the chimney contains some nitrogen and wood ashes from the autumn bonfire is another source of potash. The slow bonfire that smoulders supplies the best residue.

Inorganic

These are the 'artificials' or chemical preparations such as sulphate of ammonia, nitrate of soda, superphosphate of lime, sulphate of potash, magnesium sulphate and kainit.

Making Your Choice

There is a constant battle raging between soil experts about the dangerous long-term effects on the soil of artificials or inorganic fertilisers, and there are many gardeners who will use only the organic. It is my belief that there is a place for both organic and inorganic fertilisers.

Organics are invaluable, possessing enduring qualities, and I recommend them particularly to the beginner because they are safe. The worst that can happen should the gardener fail to follow the manufacturer's instructions and administer unsuitable doses will be that the plants will give an unbalanced performance, producing abundant leaves and no flowers or vice versa. Whereas an overdose of certain inorganics is not only harmful but deadly.

Inorganics are undoubtedly useful on occasion as a tonic or pick-me-up rather than as a soil improver. They could be compared with the magical tonic that peps up the taker for a short time without lasting benefit.

It should perhaps be stressed that inorganic fertilisers applied to poor soil lacking in organic matter are often a waste of money. If there is no humus or retentive material present to hold the chemical it will be quickly washed through the soil and lost.

Chemical fertilisers cannot replace humus.

How to Apply Manures and Fertilisers

Well-matured horse and farmyard manure and compost are best worked in with a fork when digging or double digging.

Fertilisers must be evenly scattered by hand or distributed with the aid of a fertiliser distributor, care being taken to ensure that each square yard gets its fair share, after which it can be lightly pricked in with a fork. The fertiliser should rest just below the soil's surface safe from wind and excessive rain.

When to Apply

The slower acting horse, farmyard and poultry manures and vegetable compost are best applied in the autumn or winter provided the soil is not too heavy and wet. Slow-acting organic fertilisers such as bonemeal can also be applied during autumn and winter but the quick-acting chemicals such as nitrate of soda should be applied in the spring or when the plants and vegetables are growing. They become active when the temperature rises.

A Rough Guide to the Needs of the Different Soils

Almost all types of soil welcome horse and farmyard manure, if given at the right time. Sandy soils are deficient in potash; sulphate of potash can safely be added in the spring or early summer, and carrots, onions, cauliflower, asparagus and all flowers appreciate this boost.

Sour soil which has been rendered unhealthy due to waterlogging, poor aeration and lack of cultivation will benefit if treated with quicklime, straight from the kiln.

Chalk soil is deficient in potassium, nitrogen and very often phosphorus. Clay soil has all the assets, but through lack of culture they are not always available to the plants. Experts on this soil advise an application of 1 part sulphate of ammonia, 2 oz. sulphate of potash, 2 oz. superphosphate of lime applied in the spring at the rate of $\frac{1}{2}$ lb. to every square yard. Mulching with lawn clippings is also useful in conserving moisture.

Attention All Learners

Never apply a fertiliser in any form to a dry plant or soil.

When using a fertiliser the manufacturer's instructions should be studied and followed to the letter. Doses should always be measured out; guessing is not good enough. It is a strange fact that even the meanest of men become lavish with the fertiliser tin.

There is added charm about work that is well repaid and feeding the soil is guaranteed to bring the gardener a handsome reward. It is the right food at the right time that does the trick.

Foliar Feeding

Foliar feeds, such as liquid seaweed, are sprayed on to leaves and are absorbed into the plant's system. This method of feeding a plant is particularly helpful when the root system is not working adequately after transplanting or the plant is suffering from lack of magnesium, iron or a similar vital element.

Considerable success has been achieved during the last decade by the foliar feeding of fruit trees.

LIMING

Lime is essential to most plants. Most soils contain enough for their food requirements in the form of calcium, and it is chiefly to correct any sourness or acidity in the soil resulting from constant manuring that additional lime may be required. It is also a great aid in breaking down stiff clay and encourages the bacteria and microbes to do their work.

It cleanses the soil of insects and pests and helps to control club root or 'finger and toe' disease among turnips and wallflowers.

The Romans practised alternate dunging and liming of land and through the ages the experienced farmer and gardener have followed suit.

In times past the gardener limed freely in order to make the nourishment in the soil quickly available to his plants and crops. Then he manured to replenish the larder having discovered that the adage 'lime and lime without manure, makes both farm and farmer poor' was only too true. Soil experts now caution us to beware of over-liming and not to lime as an annual routine, but point out that there is less risk of over-liming clay (which often tends to be acid).

The gardener should first find out by testing or enquiry, from someone knowledgeable on the subject, whether he is dealing with acid or alkaline soil. Plants on the whole prefer an acid to an alkaline soil and too much lime may well be responsible for pale and discoloured leaves among the strawberries, raspberries, apples and plums and scab among the potatoes. The time-honoured belief that lime is good for stone fruit has also, to some extent, gone by the board.

Watch Out for the Lime Haters

Plants vary in their tolerance of lime. Rhododendrons, azaleas, lupins and camellias are peat lovers and lime haters. On the other hand aquilegias, carnations and pinks growing on peat invariably look sorry for themselves and much prefer a limy soil.

When and Which Dressing to Apply

Lime can be applied at any time from late autumn (October) until early March. An application once in four years will usually be found adequate.

For heavy soil slaked lime should be applied in autumn or three weeks before sowing in the spring at the rate of up to 6 oz. to the square yard.

For light and sandy soil calcium carbonate, less easily washed away by the rain, should be applied three weeks before sowing.

Note: Lime should never be applied at the same time as manure or it will react and cause the loss of nitrogen. Six weeks should be allowed to elapse before using fertilisers after liming.

How to Apply Lime

The lime, perfectly dry and finely powdered, should be dusted over the land when the soil is dry.

Never dig lime deeply into the ground; it may be lightly worked into the top 1 to 2 in. of soil by fork or rake when it will be washed in by rain.

THE COMPOST HEAP

Gardeners living in a district where it is difficult to buy farmyard manure automatically become compost-minded. They proudly lead you off to see the compost heap even before introducing you to the roses.

What is Compost?

Confusion sometimes arises because the word serves two distinct meanings. Compost can either mean any mixture of peat, loam and sand used for rearing seedlings or pot plants, or a heap of vegetable matter consisting of garden and kitchen waste which will rot down and can be dug into the soil. It is the compost heap with which we are concerned here.

Size

There are strong views as to how a compost heap should be made but there is one golden rule – never build the heap too wide or air will be excluded.

The gardener should begin in a small way with a heap of 3 to 4 ft. maximum height by not more than 3 ft. wide, building on a solid floor or foundation of bricks, rubble, or coarse vegetable matter. The heap may be partially enclosed and boarded with slab timber (the outer cut of trees which is moderate in price); a brick or concrete wall on one side will make for stability. Gaps of $\frac{1}{2}$ to 1 in. should be allowed between the rough-fitting timber to provide the ventilation that is necessary.

Gardeners with a gift for do-it-yourself carpentry can arrange posts at the corners of their heap which will allow flat boards to be slipped in and out, or ready-made heavy galvanised wire containers can be obtained. In this way the heap is contained neatly but loses nothing of its value. It should be covered and protected against the rain with a polythene or galvanised iron sheet.

Some gardeners prefer to build their heap in a shallow earth pit, but this is not advisable on waterlogged soils.

Material for the Heap

The compost heap is best started in the spring. All kinds of garden and kitchen waste may be used. The householder should collect the material gradually, covering it with sacking or polythene at night until the heap is completed.

Plant waste, bracken, lawn mowings and hedge clippings (if not too woody) and all food scraps and kitchen waste (but not fat) can be included and bark fibre, rough peat and straw are invaluable additions – in fact anything that will decompose.

Leaves in moderate quantities are desirable but are inclined to mat and slow up decay and in large amounts should be caged separately, wired in with a few posts and netting.

What to Avoid

Perennial weeds with taproots should go post haste to the bonfire along with rotting apples or any plants suffering from disease, such as club root. Wood prunings should be avoided and coarse stems such as cabbage stumps should be cut in sections before being placed on the heap.

Building the Heap

Large cabbage leaves (without woody stalks) make a good floor, or a mat of coarse annual weeds is suitable for the purpose.

The gardener should build up a 6-in. layer of waste on this carpet, adding a thin layer of manure (chicken manure will do) or a dusting of any proprietary brand of compost accelerator or decomposing agent such as sulphate of ammonia. This may be covered with half an inch of soil and then a second 6 in. of waste is added, and so on until the heap is about 4 ft. in height.

The heap should be lightly watered in dry weather in order to keep it light and spongy but care must be taken not to allow it to become sodden. The waste material will gradually warm up to 62°C. (145°F.) or more. The temperature can be tested after six weeks by inserting a stick into the heap. When withdrawn this should be warm from the fermenting waste, and if steam issues from the hole so much the better.

The air flow can be increased by the insertion of two 3-in.

Constructing a compost heap. The use of slab timber with its rough edges allows through a sufficient amount of air to give good ventilation

diameter stakes, one pushed horizontally on to the solid floor, the other rising through the heap to the soil surface, acting as a 'chimney'. An earthworm here and there is a welcome sight, proving that all is well.

Once the centre of the heap has cooled off it can be turned inside out, from sides to middle. Some gardeners forego this operation and use the unfermented sides to start a new or second heap. It is ideal, of course, to have two or more compost heaps on the go.

Quality

As the material decays so the temperature falls and if the compost is kept reasonably free of rain it becomes the much sought-after brownish black humus that is just the thing to keep a plant warm in winter and cool and moist in summer. Some say that vegetable compost is superior food to stable manure in that there is no danger of it burning tender roots and the compost may well be more pest and disease resisting. Certainly no gardener can afford to be without it.

Paths

A path may be straight or curved and should lead somewhere, or at least be of service to the gardener when attending his plants. Wriggling paths or those which lead to a dead end are, as a rule, unsatisfactory.

The working gardener demands a useful, hard-wearing backbone of paths, well drained and laid on a good base. Unless paved they should be slightly raised in the centre, up to an inch or so and mounded at the crown so that water drains off properly. The badly made path is a constant source of trouble, sinking to different levels and quick to suffer from wear and tear.

Width

A garden path should be wide enough to permit two persons to walk along side by side without bumping in to each other or at least allow room for one person with a wheelbarrow. Three feet should be enough, though subsidiary paths need only be 2 ft. 6 in. wide and rock garden paths may be narrower. A drive should be at least 8 ft. wide.

Drainage

An adequate soakaway is important on heavy clay. Pipes may have to be introduced just below foundation level, preferably at the side of the path. As before, I advise the beginner to seek professional advice if extensive drainage and piping are required.

Foundations
A 6- to 10-in. layer of broken bricks, clinkers, stones or lump chalk provides a suitable porous foundation for a garden path. Good bottom drainage of this sort is essential. The sides should be built first and then the centre.

Materials
Paths can be made of various materials, the choice depending upon the budget and the suitability of the surroundings.

The path close to the house should, whenever possible, bear some relationship to the building: the red brick path marches well with the red brick house; the stone house and flagstones go happily together.

Earth-beaten Path
This makes a temporary path for spring and summer at no cost at all. A 2-in. layer of earth should be excavated, the path raked and trodden level and then beaten flat with a spade until it is 3 or 4 in. lower than the loose surface soil.

Made in the spring, the path will serve throughout the summer if given an occasional roll to keep it trim. An earth path should not be attempted on a heavy clay soil.

Ash Path
This is a popular path for the vegetable garden. The success of the ash path depends upon a sound foundation of 6 to 9 in. of clinkers. A surface of sifted ashes can then be laid which, after levelling, must be thoroughly watered in and rolled while wet.

An ash path calls for a firm edging, otherwise the ash falls away and blackens the surrounding soil, spoiling the effect.

Cement or Concrete
This material makes a useful, permanent and hard-wearing path, though not always an attractive one. It provides an excellent surface for the garage approach.

At least 6 in. of soil should be excavated, and the path then levelled and thoroughly weeded – a stout weed will break through any crack or weak spot. A good layer of rubble and clinker is then added to give a firm foundation. Planks or boards lined with greased paper should be laid on edge at the sides of the path to keep the concrete under control.

The concrete can now be mixed in proportions of one part cement to two parts of damp sand and three of shingle or gravel aggregate or, if using mixed ballast which includes sand, one part of cement to four of mixed ballast. A special compound can be used to colour the cement according to fancy.

Concrete hardens in a flash in hot weather and should not be mixed until it is needed for use. When it is laid the surface can be given a final levelling with a flat greased board and a trowel, after which it should be covered with damp sacks to prevent it drying out too quickly and cracking.

Concrete should never be laid during frosty weather.

Concrete Slabs
Home-made concrete slabs can be made in wooden moulds with the aid of a sharp trowel and a straight edge; the boards being lined with greased paper. The concrete should be cut at least half an hour before it is set. Slabs sunk in the grass or between herbs or mat-forming plants make a useful informal path of stepping stones.

Asphalt
Cold asphalt paths have become very popular in recent years; they are cheap and extremely simple to prepare. All that is required is a firm foundation over which the asphalt is poured and raked to a depth of about $\frac{1}{2}$ in. Granite chippings are then scattered over the surface and lightly rolled in. Concrete and asphalt are not attractive mediums for garden paths but they provide a good, hard-wearing surface for a drive.

The Flagged or Paved Path
There are various kinds of paving available and they make the most desirable paths of all. Paving is ideal as a pathway round the house and for forming a terrace or patio for sitting out. It also helps to prevent mud being brought into the house and trodden into carpets.

A 5-in. excavation is needed, and the foundation is then laid with clinker topped off with fine ashes or sand upon which to lay the paving stones. For greater stability the slabs may be laid in a thin layer of concrete, or fixed with a blob of cement in each corner. They should be driven into position with a maul or heavy piece of timber. It is wise to test the paving level with a straight edge and treat the ground to a weedkiller before laying, unless concrete is to be used as a foundation.

Crazy Paving
Crazy paving may be set either in sand or in a thin layer of concrete. Whatever the method, the stones must be strictly level, otherwise they are a danger to walk on. Openings between the stones can be planted with cushion plants, but if the path is to have a concrete base remember to leave pockets in the concrete to allow for planting later.

Grass Paths
A turf path is decorative but entails hard work. If the path is used much during the winter it is likely to deteriorate and, unless planks are laid over it, be unsuitable for wheelbarrow traffic.

The grass path should not be less than 2 ft. wide, otherwise mowing is difficult. The wider the grass path the more imposing and pleasing it is likely to be. (For upkeep of grass paths see Lawns p. 28.)

Brick

The brick path is an enduring investment and adds charm to the garden. Bricks must be carefully laid with the help of a spirit level and should be set in mortar to prevent movement. Brick paths can be made in fascinating designs, such as in the familiar herringbone pattern. Old bricks, mellow with age, are the ideal, but care should be taken in their selection so that sound bricks only are chosen. Those that flake or crumble should be avoided. Special paving bricks can be obtained which are thinner than normal building bricks. One word of warning – brick paths can become very slippery in wet weather.

Gravel

The old-fashioned gravel path has much to be said for it. It is a satisfactory and durable walk provided good river gravel, and not just shingle, is used. Shingle seldom settles down to give a smooth finish even under the pressure of the heaviest roller.

Six to nine inches of soil should be excavated and a foundation laid of rubble made with brick ends and clinker plus a layer of 2 to 3 in. of gravel. The last inch should be finely screened – that is, put through a sieve – and the path watered and rolled while wet.

The gravel path should be hand weeded or treated with a weedkiller; hoeing is a mistake since it is apt to destroy the surface.

Last Word

Do not make more paths than you need. They take up valuable space in a small garden and their upkeep is considerable.

Planting

When new plants have to be put in and old plants replanted the aim should be to move them with as little disturbance as possible, to avoid shock to the plant and check to growth.

Planting Times

Deciduous trees and shrubs – those which lose their leaves in winter – are best planted from early November until the end of March; evergreens in September and October or from March to April, and most herbaceous plants from October to March.

Container-grown plants from nurseries or garden centres can be planted out at any time, even when in flower, provided they are well soaked prior to planting and the ground is in suitable condition to receive them, not sodden with rain nor bound by frost.

Preparing Soil and Plant

A spade should be used for planting the big plants and a trowel for the small. The ground should be prepared well ahead of planting so that the soil and the well-rotted manure or compost worked into it has time to settle. The soil must be made as suitable as possible for the plant, and careful thought given to spacing, taking into account the ultimate size of the plant and bearing in mind that poplars and large trees can be a menace to house foundations.

In a dry spell, ground where trees or shrubs are to be planted should be soaked with a hose several days previously.

Planting should be done as soon as possible after the plant's arrival. If a plant has been lifted and for some reason the work has to be delayed, heel it in a trench covering the roots with earth, afterwards watering if necessary.

A plant arriving when the soil is frostbound can remain in its packing for a week or so in a frost-proof place (the spare bedroom will do), provided the top of the package is opened so that the air can circulate.

Choose a fine day when the soil is just damp, neither wet nor frostbound. Prepare the plant by watering it generously the night before planting. This will prevent the soil from falling away from the roots. The planting hole, more wide than deep, should be large enough to accommodate the plant roots comfortably at the same depth as previously planted. This can be judged by the soil mark left on the main stem. When fully extended, roots should barely touch the sides and bottom of the hole.

Cut back any broken or damaged roots. Lower the plant into the hole and spread out the roots both vertically and laterally. Don't make the mistake of forcing them down into a narrow hole. Standard trees should be attached to a stake and this should be put in first as it might damage the roots if added later.

Planting a small herbaceous plant with a trowel

Loose soil and a sprinkling of fine compost should be worked in round the plant and in between the roots. The soil should then be rammed home with the handle of the trowel or by treading with the feet. Continue filling and treading until the hole is filled and then water the plant in to settle the roots.

The new arrivals should not be allowed to dry out before and immediately after planting: they are particularly vulnerable in a dry spring.

The beginner should choose plants which do well in his neighbourhood and which will thrive in the soil and climate he has to offer. It is foolish to try to grow rhododendrons or heather on lime for they hate it and there are many others that have their strong dislikes. So if you are gardening on alkaline soil why not instead choose plants which will thrive in alkaline conditions, such as a *Daphne mezereum* or hypericums? It is important to ensure that you have nature on your side.

Weeding

Weeds are every gardener's lot, and the old saying 'one year's seeding means seven years' weeding' is very true. They can be broadly divided into annual and perennial weeds.

The annuals are not difficult to eradicate but the trouble is that groundsel, Shepherd's Purse and others flower and seed so fast that they have to be dealt with promptly and regularly. The fleshy tap-rooted perennials, the dandelions and docks, spread rapidly either by their roots or seed. Couch grass, ground elder, and bindweed (convolvulus) are three outstandingly difficult subjects to get rid of.

Hand weeding is effectual if tiresome. The beginner will soon get to know the difference between the weed and the plant seedling. Meanwhile he would be wise to sow flower

and vegetable seed in lines so that they can be easily distinguished.

Hoeing with a very sharp Dutch hoe is a good way of chopping off the weed's foliage just below soil level. The constant removal of leaves will weaken the root system, and eventually exhaust it. Weeds left intact on the surface soil will wither in the sun but are best gathered up and burnt or they may re-establish themselves after a shower.

Mulching and the planting of ground-cover plants are effective in smothering weeds and modern chemical weed-killers are also a help. Of these paraquat is one of the most useful, entering leaves and stems on contact but becoming inactive once it touches the soil. It can therefore be used safely among plants in the border provided it does not come in contact with their foliage, and is best applied through a sprinkle bar fitted to a watering-can to avoid splashing.

For paths and drives simazine is very effective. It controls many germinating weeds, remaining active in the ground for months, and it does not spread laterally.

Selective weedkillers which destroy some types of weeds and not others (such as mecoprop against clover), are helpful and the menacing bindweed can be controlled by the hormone solution 2,4-D. If a bindweed shoot is dangled in this solution the chemical will be carried back to the enemy's roots. Unfortunately this brushwood killer is not so effective in controlling ground elder.

Sodium chlorate is a powerful and cheap mass killer. It is, however, highly inflammable and must be used with care. Safer forms containing a fire depressant can be obtained, and must be used strictly in accordance with the manufacturer's instructions. Treated ground must be left unplanted for six months after use. This chemical is particularly suitable for clearing paths and neglected vacant plots.

What, a novice may ask, is the price of a garden free from weeds? The answer is eternal vigilance.

A sprinkle-bar attachment enables weedkiller to be watered directly on to weeds avoiding the foliage of plants

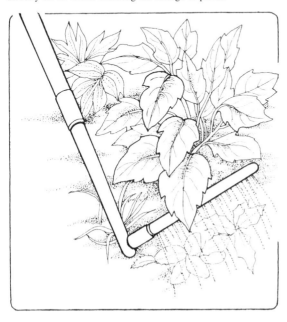

Summer bedding plants contribute to the brilliant display of colour in this town garden

Pruning

There are gardeners frightened to cut a twig; others who find the urge to use their secateurs irresistible. There is a certain confusion about the whole business of pruning.

First I should point out that a number of shrubs and trees do not need pruning at all and cutting them back is likely to spoil their natural habit and beauty. Evergreens require little pruning. Shrubs from the nursery are usually well shaped and will need little pruning during their first year.

When to Prune
As a general rule, summer-flowering shrubs should be pruned in February or March and the winter and spring shrubs immediately after flowering.

The knife should be used to improve the shape of a shrub and keep its growth within bounds. Diseased wood should be cut out along with over-vigorous branches. This will encourage weak and new growth.

How to Prune
Use secateurs for the smaller branches and a pruning saw for those over 1 in. in diameter. Using a knife calls for practice and skill and is not an easy tool for the beginner.

Unless your tools are really sharp, making a clean cut, you will do more harm than good.

Prune back to healthy wood, and if possible to a bud pointing in the direction you wish the plant to grow. Make a sloping or vertical cut and paint the wound if larger than $\frac{1}{2}$ in. across with a good wound dressing.

There are special long-arm pruners for reaching tall branches while a pruning handsaw will be needed for the thicker limbs of large trees. Cuts must be made flush with the main stem, first sawing a quarter of the way through from below the bough before sawing through from the top.

Old and neglected trees and shrubs call for drastic treatment even if it means foregoing the current year's bloom. Shock to the plant may be reduced by treating a limited number of branches yearly while shortening the remainder.

Perhaps I should mention that certain plants such as *Daphne mezereum* and certain brooms when mature and aged are outstandingly sensitive to the knife and should be allowed to grow fancy free. Pruning of roses and fruit will be found under their specific headings.

Should the gardener be in doubt as to whether to prune or not, let him put his knife away: it is wiser to prune too little than to prune too much.

Propagation

SEEDS
Growing from seed is the cheapest method of propagating plants, particularly when a number are wanted. Not all seed comes true, either to its parents or the pictures on the packet, but there is always the exciting (but distant) chance that the gardener may rear a new and outstanding variety. The sower must remember that moisture, warmth and air are vital for germination and once seeds have germinated light is essential for the seedlings. He will find growing from seed a fascinating occupation.

Marking out a seed drill with a pointed stick

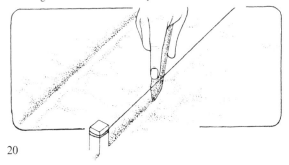

Sowing Outdoors
Hardy annuals can be sown out of doors in March or April and many perennials in late spring or summer.

Biennials can be sown in the semi-shade in May or June and transplanted at least once before being installed in their final position for flowering the following year. Many hardy perennials, shrubs and trees can also be grown from seed sown in the ground out of doors, or in pots or boxes.

The seed bed must be dug and raked to a fine tilth a few weeks before sowing, and stones and lumps removed. Sowing is best done when the soil is slightly moist and on a still day. A drill—a trench $\frac{1}{2}$ in. deep—should be made with the corner of the hoe, or for very small seed a pointed stick will serve the purpose. A garden line stretched between two stakes will ensure that the drill is drawn straight. On very heavy soil a sprinkling of damp peat or leafmould at the bottom of the trench is helpful. The seed should now be sprinkled into the drill through a corner of the packet or distributed evenly by finger and thumb.

Some gardeners prefer to scatter seeds at random or sow them in groups known as stations. Whatever the method the seed should be sown as thinly as possible to reduce the tiresome job of thinning out later on. Large seeds such as nasturtiums should be sown singly 6 to 8 in. apart and covered with about 1½ in. of soil.

Some seeds such as sweet peas and lupins have hard coats and to assist germination it is advisable to chip them with a sharp knife or file, breaking the skin on the side opposite the seed scar.

Small seeds should be covered with only a suspicion of sieved soil and lightly firmed to a flat surface. Brushwood twigs can be laid across the seed bed as a protection against birds, cats and dogs, but should be removed once the seedlings have come through the soil. Annuals sown in situ can be allowed to grow through the twigs.

Sowing Indoors
The half-hardy annuals are sown in early spring in the greenhouse, being too tender to grow out of doors.

They can be sown in pots or pans 2 to 3 in. deep, or in wooden or plastic seed trays with drainage holes. These should be filled with a finely sieved loam and a sprinkling of sharp sand, or better still, John Innes Seed Compost.

Once sown the pan should be watered with a can fitted with a fine rose. Another way of watering seeds and small seedlings is to immerse the pan up to its rim in a trough of water until the moisture has darkened the surface of the compost. The pan is then covered with glass and a sheet of brown paper. The moisture must be wiped from the glass daily. Once the seed germinates both glass and paper must be removed.

When the seedlings have formed their second pair of leaves following the first pair of seed leaves they can be pricked out into pots and boxes and kept shaded for twenty four hours.

Seedlings
Seedlings should be hardened off by increased ventilation, or preferably placed in a frame, to prepare them gradually for outdoor conditions, before being planted in the garden in their flowering positions.

The first thinning out should be done when the seedlings can be comfortably handled and a second and third thinning carried out if necessary before the youngsters get drawn and leggy. Many seedlings will transplant if the move is made at an early stage on a dullish day, but there are some plants such as the poppy that cannot be transplanted. In cold areas, cloches placed over the young biennials or perennials in late October are often a life saver.

Saving Seed
Gardeners intending to save seed should harvest fruit or seed heads when dry and lay them in a tray in an airy place to finish their ripening. Later on the seeds should be cleaned by rolling them down blotting paper or a rough-textured cloth or passing through a fine-meshed sieve. They should then be stored in an airtight tin until the following sowing season.

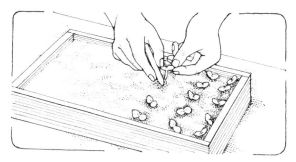

Pricking out seedlings using a small dibber. The young seedlings should be held by the seed leaf, not by the stem

It is not advisable to save the seed from the carefully bred F_1 varieties since they will not come true to type. These plants are hybrids which need special pollination and must therefore be bought afresh each year from the professional seedsman.

CUTTINGS
A cutting is a portion of stem, leaf or root taken from a plant and prepared in such a way that it will grow into a new plant.

Softwood and Half-ripe Cuttings
Herbaceous plants such as the delphinium, lupin and dahlia, and small subjects such as the pink, lobelia or ageratum are easily increased from softwood cuttings. Chrysanthemum cuttings are best taken from basal shoots growing directly from the roots at just below ground level.

The gardener should select semi-ripened growth, not sappy or hollow-stemmed shoots. In the case of the geranium and other nodal cuttings (that is, jointed stems) the cut should be made immediately below a bud or joint.

Summer prunings of aubrieta and alpine phlox will provide useful cuttings.

Making the Cutting
A short jointed cutting of 2 to 5 in. taken from the top of the shoot should be chosen and the leaves removed from a third of its length leaving three to four pairs of leaves at the top. Any buds below the leaves should be rubbed out. The base of each cutting should then be dipped in a hormone rooting powder, available from garden shops.

A clean pot should now be filled with a loam and peat or vermiculite compost with a generous top layer of silver sand, or John Innes Seed Compost, and the cuttings inserted to a depth of one third of their length round the side of the pot, close to the rim, and watered in.

The cuttings will be encouraged to strike if kept in a close and humid atmosphere, such as in a frame, or covered with a polythene bag secured by a rubber band. Enough water should be given to keep the soil slightly moist.

When new leaves appear the cutting's future will be assured and once showing itself well rooted it is ready for potting up into an individual 3-in. pot.

Hardwood Cuttings

Many shrubs and soft fruit bushes can be increased by this method. Well-ripened shoots of the previous year's growth 8 to 10 in. long should be chosen, the top trimmed with a slanting cut just above a bud and the base with a horizontal cut made just below a node or joint.

Hardwood cuttings may be rooted in a cold frame or in the open ground; a shaded position at the north side of a wall or hedge is ideal.

September and October, while the soil is still warm, is a good time for taking such cuttings which should then be inserted upright to a depth of about one third of their length in a trench sprinkled with sand. Care must be taken to ensure that they do not dry out.

Potting up should not be hurried; it may be the following autumn before the cuttings are well rooted and ready for planting.

Root Cuttings

Anchusa, anemone, the oriental poppy and other thick-rooted herbaceous plants are best increased by root cuttings in spring or early summer.

Roots of the parent plant should be cleaned after lifting and cut into lengths of 1 to 3 in. They should be laid horizontally in a deep seed box filled with loam, peat and sand and lightly covered over with the same mixture finely sieved. The box can then be placed in a sheltered place in the garden and covered by a sheet of glass until shoots appear.

Water moderately and transplant later to a nursery bed.

Leaf Cuttings

Fibrous-rooted Rex begonias and gloxinias lend themselves to propagation by leaf cuttings. The main veins of a leaf should be nicked with a razor blade, laid flat in a seed box or pot on damp, sandy compost, and pinned in place with hairpins.

The leaf should then be placed in a shaded frame or greenhouse and covered with a sheet of glass. Roots soon form from the incisions and if a close, damp atmosphere is maintained, new plants will develop.

Internodal Cuttings

There are plants, among them the clematis, from which

Dividing the roots of a herbaceous perennial by using two forks back to back and levering them apart

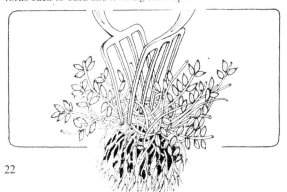

internodal cuttings can be taken, an incision being made between two joints.

Heel Cuttings

When a cutting is taken from a plant by pulling a side shoot away with a downward pull so that a small strip of bark is attached it is described as a heel cutting.

Many cuttings appear to strike more readily if they possess a heel of older wood attached to their base.

Irishman's Cutting

This is a shoot pulled away from the parent plant with a root or two attached. Strictly speaking, it is a small division rather than a cutting. The term is used humorously in gardening circles.

LAYERING

Shrubs presenting long, pliable shoots of the previous year's growth can be encouraged to root by bending them down to the soil. A slanting cut or a restricting twist half-way through the underside of the shoot should be made at the point where it touches the ground.

Non-flowering shoots should be chosen for layering carnations and soft-growing plants. In the case of carnations they should be slit through a joint, and the tip of the layered shoot staked to a split cane.

A mound of leafmould, sand and peat should be built up to meet the incision made in the stem. The cut may be slightly opened and treated to hormone powder, pressed an inch deep into the mound of soil, and pegged down with bent wire. It is advisable to mark the spot with a stake to avoid disturbing the layered shoot during routine weeding.

Rhododendrons, clematis, wisteria, lilac, and rambler roses are some of the shrubs easily persuaded to co-operate in this method of propagation.

Hard-wooded shoots may take over a year to form an independent root system, and the gardener should not be in a hurry to sever them from the parent plant.

Budding and Grafting

These propagating operations are for the more experienced and green-fingered gardener.

DIVISION

This is the easiest way of increasing Michaelmas daisies, heleniums, geums and other herbaceous perennials.

Clumps can be lifted in the autumn when growth is dying down, or in the spring, just before the plant begins growing, split up into several pieces and replanted.

Large clumps which are tough and difficult to divide may be levered apart by pushing two border forks back to back through the centre of the plant and forcing the handles outwards in different directions. If necessary a knife can be used to reduce the divisions to a reasonable size.

Colour harmony is important in the herbaceous border

The aim should be to replant sections of young, outside growth while discarding the tired, worn-out centre of the clump. The younger growth gives a superior performance to the old.

Some herbaceous plants, among them Michaelmas daisies, respond to division annually, whereas others such as the peony do best when left undisturbed for four or five years.

Day-by-day Chores

The gardener is more than a part-time worker. For good gardening, like good cooking, takes not only skill but time.

Soil Aeration
Soil must be kept aerated, that is to say kept open with a fork or hoe, otherwise it tends to become compacted and unfit for plant habitation, but every care must be taken when using a fork not to injure tender roots.

Tidying
Trimming or pinching a plant into shape when shoots are young will save hard pruning later on.

Deadheading
Deadheading is an important operation particularly where annuals are concerned. By preventing the formation of a seed head the plant is encouraged to produce more flowers.

Staking
There is a knack in staking and in giving a plant support without spoiling its appearance. The floppy plant should be staked at an early stage to protect it from damage by wind, rain, and root rock.

Pea sticks give light support without ruining the plant's appearance. Individual bamboo sticks must be provided for delphiniums and others with heavier stems and wooden stakes may be required for dahlias in a windswept district.

The worn-out twigs from birch brooms provide excellent light support for annuals.

Fertilisers
The best time to apply fertiliser is before the flowering season. A plant enjoying a well-deserved rest after flowering should not be flogged with stimulating chemicals.

Mulching
A 2-in. layer of well-rotted animal manure, compost, spent hops, or lawn mowings should be applied in May when the soil is warming up, and the sap rising fast. The mulch put on after a good watering or a downfall of rain to conserve moisture is often a life saver. It also helps to defeat weeds.

Watering
When watering, the gardener should be generous: dribs and drabs merely stimulate thirsty roots near the surface without satisfying them. So when using the hose make it a good soak. Once watering is started it must be continued regularly until rain falls.

Removal
When bulbs, such as daffodils, tulips and other spring flowers are over they are invariably in the way but the foliage must be allowed to die back naturally, either where they have flowered or moved to a trench out of sight. Annuals may be discarded when they have completed their year's cycle. Perennials should be cut back in late autumn in warm districts but dead stems may be allowed to remain in cold areas as winter protection. Some perennials will give a second performance if cut back immediately after flowering.

Failure
When a young plant dies, a gardener often has a feeling of guilt. With good reason? Possibly it was his fault. Maybe it was planted in a hurry, or allowed to dry out during the spring winds, or planted loosely so that it suffered root rock?

On the other hand the plant may have suffered a rough journey or have been seriously delayed by rail or post. It is always possible that the plant was in poor shape even before it left the nursery, or maybe the weather was against the plant? It is often difficult to put a finger on the reason for the failure.

By all means let the nurseryman know that the plant has died, remembering that the fault may not be his.

Successful Timing
The slow coach must wake up and get busy, nature will not wait for him. Timing is as important in the garden as anywhere else, if not more so.

Water the thirsty plant before it wilts.

Cut the lawn before it gets too long; two light cuts are less time taking than one when grass is overgrown, and kinder to the lawn.

Stake plants early rather than late. Bent stalks seldom straighten out.

Cut hedges when growth is soft. It's so much easier.

Feed plants before they show signs of starvation.

Prick out all seedlings in good time before they become drawn and leggy.

Spray greenfly on sight. Here, a stitch in time saves more than nine.

Spray or dust as a preventive measure against mildew, before it arrives.

Deadhead daily to encourage flowering. Annuals first.

Weed as you walk and don't give the weeds a chance of seeding.

And keep a constant watch.

Pests and Diseases

Nearly all plants are from time to time attacked by pests and diseases. Weak, sickly, starved, and ill-conditioned plants invite the enemy. If the highest standard of hygiene is carried out in the garden the incidence both of pests and diseases will be reduced.

Ants
These small insects damage the roots of young plants by underground tunnelling.

Control: An insecticide based on BHC or pyrethrum will control these pests.

Aphids
Greenfly is the most common of all garden pests. Nasturtiums are menaced by black fly.

Controls: Menazon, a systemic insecticide—that is, one which is taken into the sap of the plant. It is harmful to humans and animals. Derris is less toxic and harmless to humans and animals, although poisonous to fish. Pyrethrum is non-poisonous both to humans and warm-blooded animals, and being 'safe' is a wise choice. Derris and pyrethrum are contact insecticides, acting on contact with the body of the insect.

Caterpillars
The larvae of butterflies and moths may be sprayed or dusted with derris and any survivor promptly dealt with by finger and thumb.

Cats
Control: A sniff of ammonia plus a bedding of prickly thistle around the squatter's favourite plant will discourage visitors. Garden pepper and repellent preventive spray in aerosol form are helpful.

Cuckoo Spit
The larvae of the froghopper, yellow or green in colour, is not a serious pest.

Control: Quickly cleared by removing spittle with warm soapy water and afterwards spraying with derris, or by picking off by hand.

Dogs
There are various proprietary dog repellents including a specially treated cord to keep dogs away.

Earwigs
This pest is especially damaging to the dahlia, eating flowers and foliage at night.

Control: Earwigs can be trapped in upturned pots filled with hay, placed on canes above the plant, and shaken out over a bucket of water in the morning. Earwigs and woodlice can also be controlled by applications of BHC.

Eelworms
Attacking the roots of certain plants, these pests are invisible to the naked eye, and almost impossible to eradicate.

Control: Affected plants are best burnt and the ground left vacant for three or more years. Phlox, chrysanthemums, primulas and campanulas are vulnerable.

Slugs
Control: A number of metaldehyde and bran products are available. A dressing of sharp cinders round the plants hinders slug progress.

Chlorosis
A yellowing of foliage due to chlorophyll deficiency.

Control: A generous feed of organic manure or a foliar feed of liquid seaweed, particularly if shortage of iron is responsible, will usually put things right.

Damping Off
Seedlings under glass are vulnerable to stem rot caused by fungi.

Control: The use of John Innes Seed Compost or sterilised soil will minimise the risk of disease. The use of Cheshunt compound before sowing and at pricking-out time is a safeguard. Good ventilation, without draughts, is essential.

Virus Diseases
Dahlias, petunias, zinnias, nasturtiums and many border plants suffer from a virus that travels in the sap, resulting in distortions or markings. Many of the wilt conditions are due to virus for which there is no known cure. All plants suffering severely from the disease are best burnt and a watch kept for aphids that act as virus carriers.

The gardener's knife and fingers can carry virus from plant to plant.

Part II

Plants and Garden Features

Clematis Ville de Lyon and Perle d'Azur

The Lawn

The gardener who specialises in a smooth green lawn is handsomely rewarded, for he will have something pleasant to look at the whole year through. The lawn is a permanent feature and nothing will show off flowers more favourably than a richly coloured sward.

Having once inherited an ill-conditioned lawn I know it to be a constant expense and irritation until groomed or re-made.

Soil

A fibrous loam is ideal for lawn making. Sandy and poor soil will need an addition of well-rotted manure or peat nicely mixed in before sowing or laying turf. Heavy clay can be improved by introducing sand or peat but lime should not be used unless the ground is really acid, as it will encourage the growth of clover and the coarser grasses.

As a rule it is only necessary to dig to the depth of a spade when preparing for sowing or turfing.

Drainage

It is impossible to make a satisfactory lawn if the drainage is at fault, and on very heavy land the gardener may have to double dig, taking care not to bring the subsoil to the top. If the soil is clay and the site of the lawn is flat and spongy, frequently becoming waterlogged, a pipe system leading to a soakaway may have to be provided, but advice should be sought before this is attempted. Another way of improving drainage is to remove the top layer of soil to a depth of 6 to 8 in. and add a layer of hard rubble, together with peat and coarse sand, before replacing the surface soil.

Preparation

The site should be thoroughly dug and the ground cleared of perennial weeds. This should be done as long as possible before the date of sowing, at least a month and possibly three or four, to allow the ground time to settle.

Slightly sloping lawns are more attractive than flat ones, but a level surface is necessary for the smooth running of the mower. For a truly level surface the area must be checked with the aid of a spirit level and board, a length of wood about 9 ft. long, 4 in. wide and $\frac{3}{4}$ in. thick.

A peg should be driven into the centre of the area so that its top is at the required level of the lawn. A second peg is then hammered in about 8 ft. away so that its top is at exactly the same level as the first. This can be checked accurately by laying the board across the two pegs with the spirit level on top of it, and adjusting the depth of the second peg until the bubble of the spirit level is exactly centred. The third peg is then driven in 8 ft. away on the other side of the first, and this operation is repeated at four more points at equal distances from the first peg in compass fashion.

On uneven ground some of the pegs will now be up to their necks in soil, others half exposed, though the tops of all of them will be at the same level. Soil can now be moved from the higher points to the lower until finally all the pegs are exposed at the same height above the ground.

The rough clods of soil are broken down with a fork and a pre-dressing of a reputable lawn fertiliser should be applied at $1\frac{1}{2}$ to 2 oz. per square yard or bonemeal at 2 to 3 oz. per square yard and worked in to the top 2 in. with fork and rake.

After the ground has been well broken up and levelled the soil should be firmed. This is done by treading, keeping your feet together and taking the shortest of steps, toe following heel. Once the soil has been reduced to a fine tilth, unwanted bumps can be raked and smoothed away. A final raking should be given with the handle held low, to reduce the tilth to seed-bed quality. The small furrows left by the rake are helpful if sowing seed.

Sowing versus Turfing

The gardener making a new lawn has to decide whether to sow seed or lay turf. Sowing seed is harder work requiring more care and time, but is cheaper. The best time to sow in the South is in late August or early September; in the North sowing is best done during the last weeks of August. Failing summer sowing, the middle of April is the best period.

Choice of Seed

Grass seed plays an important part in the seedsman's business and he is always ready to help the gardener with advice. But he must be told as much as possible about conditions – the soil and aspect, sun and shade, and the use to which the lawn is to be put. Has it to stand up to hard and rough wear, or is it to be just a pleasing green turf?

Fifty parts Chewing's Fescue, 20 parts Creeping Red Fescue and 30 parts Brown Top is a generally satisfactory mixture, but given the particular requirements of the lawn you wish to grow the modern seedsman may improve on this.

How to Sow

Seed should be sown on a fine, calm day when the soil is neither wet nor over dry. It can be done by hand or by using a seed or fertiliser distributor. The site is divided into 1-yd. wide strips and a container used to gauge the correct amount for each section, or the beginner may prefer to use a wooden frame 1 sq. yd. in area for greater accuracy.

Seed should be sown at the rate of $1\frac{1}{2}$ to 2 oz. per square yard, remembering that very thin sowing gives the weeds more elbow room. It is wise to divide and weigh the seed into lots so that each square yard gets its fair share. Those who find difficulty in scattering evenly may find it helpful to mix the seed first with four times the quantity of dry sand.

Seed must be lightly covered with soil using the back of the fork to close the furrows left by the rake. It must not be covered too deeply, not more than half an inch, or the grass may not grow through.

On light soils – but not on clay – a final touch can be given by rolling it to help settle the surface, using the roller of a very light mower and pulling the machine towards you so that the blades are disengaged.

Protection from Birds
Seed treated with a bird repellent is available, but it takes a lot to defeat the sparrow. Bird repellent sprays are soon washed away by heavy showers, and black cotton, passed criss-cross between small stakes, twigs or firewood, an old-fashioned dodge, is probably the best protection.

Germination
Given seven to ten fine days the seed should be seen to sprout. Weeds, the gardener's lot, will also develop and should be pulled up in their infancy. The lawn should be kept free from fallen debris, and any bare patches resown. When the grass is 2 to 3 in. high it may be mown for the first time with razor-sharp blades set as high as they will go. If the box is removed from the machine the mowings will provide a helpful mulch.

In about six weeks the gardener should have a lawn, and in six months be on his way to possessing the much desired emerald sward.

Turfing
Turfing, a more expensive method of making a lawn, can be undertaken during autumn, winter or spring and provides a ready-made effect. Autumn is a wise choice as there is less risk of drought at that season.

Turf varies tremendously in quality and it is important to buy from a reputable source. Turves should, if possible, be inspected before buying. They should be immaculate, reasonably weed-free rolls of either 18 in. by 1 ft. or, on occasion, 1 ft. square and $1\frac{1}{4}$ to $1\frac{1}{2}$ in. thick. Whatever their shape they must be uniform in size.

Laying the Turves
The site should be prepared as for seed sowing. If the turves are flattened out on a table and weeds removed before laying you will save many a backache later on.

A line of turves should now be placed on the ground and beaten flat with a flat piece of wood fitted with a central handle, or lightly flattened with the back of a spade. A second line of turves should then be placed close up to the first line, the joints staggered as in bricklaying. The gardener should stand on a plank laid across the freshly prepared ground while doing this work.

The turves should be placed tightly against each other to avoid any gaps. Any chinks between them should be filled with good light loam. When turfing a slope it may be necessary to peg the turves in position.

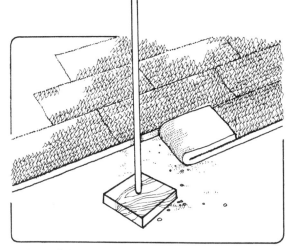

Laying turf, showing the turves bonded like bricks in a wall and the wooden rammer for firming them in place

CARE AND MAINTENANCE

Mowing
In summer, after 'topping' and during the fast growing season, the new lawn will benefit by being mown twice a week. This prevents the rye and other unwanted grasses flowering and seeding themselves. If the lawn is regularly mown coarse grass gradually dies out. The grass should never be cut lower than $\frac{1}{2}$ in. high.

Mow along the length of the lawn at the first mowing, across at the next, and finally diagonally from corner to corner. In this way coarse grass and weeds cannot escape the blades and the finer grasses will be encouraged to spread.

As autumn approaches the blades of the mower should be set higher and the grass cut less frequently, until by the end of October regular mowing will no longer be necessary. A last mow on a dry warm day can be given in November but the grass should be left about 2 in. long to provide protection for the roots during the winter.

Choosing a Mower
The choice of mower will depend on your garden budget and the size of your garden. If your lawn is more than a quarter of an acre in size a motor or battery-type electric mower will be necessary, and the owner of a small patch, who wants to spare himself the effort of pushing, may prefer one of the small mains electric models as an alternative to the hand-propelled machine.

There is a large range of hand-propelled mowers and I would advise a beginner to visit Chelsea, Southport and county flower shows or some of the big garden centres where a number of these machines are on view and can be handled. The double roller cylinder model appears to give the best finish.

Of the power-driven mowers the battery electric are very popular. For the housewife mowing the lawn in her spare time there are comparatively quiet models rather similar

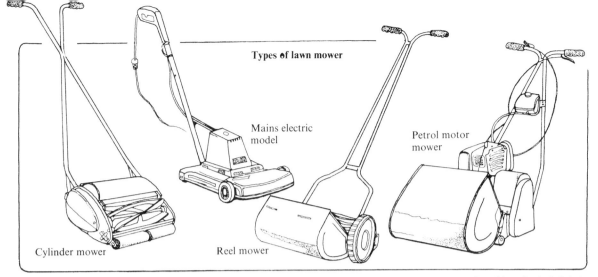

Types of lawn mower

Mains electric model

Petrol motor mower

Cylinder mower

Reel mower

to a vacuum cleaner which are fairly trouble free. One model, operating on the principle of the hovercraft air cushion, responds to the lightest touch.

The petrol-engined mowers are for the mechanically minded man with a large area to mow. The rotary motor mower that cuts both long and short grass may not give a perfect finish but is a blessing for the gardener with an informal lawn of the Continental type, where spring bulbs have been naturalised.

Here are a few tips about maintenance.

Always wipe the mower down after use and keep the blades sharp. If the machine has been used in damp grass it may be necessary to clean both the cylinder and plate. Overhaul the mower at the end of the season or send it to be serviced. It will receive better attention in the autumn than in the spring rush.

Warning: Accidents with mowers and mechanical cultivators are far too common. Switch off the power before attending to engine or blades. Strong leather shoes or boots should be worn when using a heavy machine. Canvas shoes are a menace.

Edging

Edges must be kept trim with sharp, long-handled edging shears which are held strictly parallel to the edge of the lawn. If this is done frequently the chore of picking up the clippings will be unnecessary.

An uneven edge can be straightened with an edging iron, using twine stretched between two pegs as a guide-line. Make an outward slanting rather than a vertical cut, otherwise the edges of the lawn will tend to break down when trodden upon. Badly broken-down edges are best cut out and the turf turned round and relaid so that the broken edge will merge with the established lawn.

Brushing and Raking

Brushing and raking with a spring-toothed rake will get rid of worm casts and the accumulated debris of dead and decaying material and prevent it forming a mat which would choke the grass roots. It also helps to expose the

stems of weeds to the mower. Brushing is helpful in encouraging young grass.

Rolling

Unless the lawn is being used for games which require a particularly even surface, rolling with a heavy roller should not be necessary, and can compact the turf. The rolling received from the lightweight roller of an average cylinder mower with the blades disengaged should be quite sufficient. The object of rolling is to encourage the grass roots to spread, not to flatten the surface. Rolling should not be done when the ground is wet or after a frost.

Aeration

By September the turf may have become compacted from constant use, particularly if the soil is heavy, and will benefit from a spiking. This can be done with a hollow-tined fork or special spiking tool, or quite simply with an ordinary garden fork. The fork is thrust in at 2 to 3 in. depth and the turf raised slightly, this being repeated every 4 to 6 in. all over the lawn.

Watering

Regular and generous watering must be given during the summer, particularly during a drought, and a sprinkler is a must if a perfect lawn is wanted. Watering in dribs and drabs does more harm than good: the lawn should be given a good soaking and allowed almost to dry out before being soaked again.

Feeding the Lawn

Lawn enthusiasts give the turf an early summer dressing of a compound fertiliser but the majority of gardeners will content themselves with feeding in spring and autumn. The beginner would be wise to ask advice as to which fertiliser would best suit his soil and the nurseryman is only too

Cool colours and still water create a delightful haven in the heart of a busy city. Even in a small area a pool can be a most effective garden feature

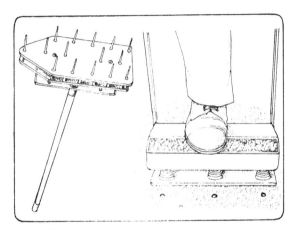

Two methods of aerating a lawn: a spiking tool and a hollow-tined aerator

happy to be consulted if given full particulars. Whatever the fertiliser chosen it is essential to follow the manufacturer's instructions, measuring out in exact quantities.

The tonic is best applied before a shower of rain or in liquid form. The fertiliser may be thrown into the air two or three feet above the grass so that it falls evenly like dust, afterwards being lightly brushed in or, when feeding a large lawn, spread evenly by means of a wheeled fertiliser distributor.

Too much fertiliser at any one time may scorch or even kill the grass: it should never be rolled in or applied to a dry soil.

The first feed should be given early in April. There are a number of reputable feeds: some are a combined stimulant and weedkiller, or a complete fish manure plus a seaweed dressing is suitable for a small lawn.

A topdressing of equal parts peat or leafmould and sieved fibrous loam with a generous sprinkling of hoof and horn will bring new life to a dull lawn. Good sifted soil with a dash of complete fertiliser acts as a refresher, and a top-dressing of sharp sand is an effective antidote against rank grass and a lack of aeration.

By September the grass may well be hungry, needing as much if not more feeding than other plants, having been impoverished, if not exhausted, by constant mowing. A home-made or reputable bulk organic dressing should be given, such as 2 to 3 oz. of complete fish manure plus 8 to 16 oz. of compost or peat per square yard, and well brushed in. Alternatively, a lawn fertiliser can be obtained for autumn application which contains a higher proportion of phosphorus and potassium than of nitrogen, since too much nitrogen at this time of the year will encourage lush growth and disease in winter.

If the lawn is in good condition a topdressing of loam, peat and sand finely sieved will be adequate.

Repairs

Autumn is the best time for carrying out repairs and small hollows in the lawn can be levelled up by filling in with a finely sieved compost until an even surface is reached. If the hollows are deep or bumps pronounced the turf must be rolled back, soil added or removed, and the turf then replaced.

Bare and brown patches should be cut out and returfed or seeded. Edgings must be kept neatly trimmed, and where the sides have been trodden and broken down extra soil can be added to build them up.

Weeds

Weeds have an unfortunate way of springing up with the newly sown grass. This is usually due to the ground not having been left fallow long enough for the perennial weeds to be eliminated before sowing.

Pearlwort and the more resistant weeds can be dealt with by spot treatment using a selective weedkiller from an aerosol or puffer pack. Coarse tufts of grass should be cross-slashed with a sharp knife or edging iron, and daisies are best treated with lawn sand or hormone selective weedkillers.

The growth of clover is usually the result of too much phosphate or of the lawn having been allowed to dry out. The grass should be regularly watered in dry weather, raked before mowing so that the blades cut the creeping stems of clover, and, if severely infested, treated to applications of a selective weedkiller.

Lawn sand, applied at 4 oz. to the square yard in dry weather, will dispose of many of the broad-leaved weeds. It may turn the lawn a trifle black but there is no need to be disturbed – provided an overdose has not been given, colour will soon return and the grass will grow through more strongly than ever, since the chemical ingredients of lawn sand are fertilisers.

The gardener should get to know the enemy: the plantain, buttercup, yarrow, chickweed and the rest. They can all be dealt with by selective weedkillers: the nurseryman will identify weed specimens and advise you how they are best destroyed.

Selective weedkiller is best applied on a fine, windless day, preferably just before a shower of rain, but if there is no rainfall it should be watered in or it may scorch the young grass. Lawn sand, on the other hand, should be applied in dry weather, since to be effective it should be left lying for some time on the broad leaves of weeds.

Moss can be temporarily controlled by mercurised lawn sand, but it will inevitably return if the lawn is compacted, badly drained, impoverished or very shady. Raking it out may result in the scattering of spores and spreading growth.

PESTS AND DISEASES

Leatherjackets

These are probably the worst of the lawn pests that attack grass roots in late summer and autumn. The area should be soaked with water and covered with sacking or polythene overnight to keep out the air. This will bring any leatherjackets present to the surface, when they can be destroyed.

Worms

Worms are useful in the soil but if too numerous and troublesome the lawn should be dressed with mowrah meal or chlordane. Mowrah meal brings the worms to the surface and there is then the unpleasant business of sweeping up the corpses. Chlordane kills them below ground but it is a concentrate that must be handled with care.

Fusarium Patch

There are a number of diseases of grass caused by fungi, one of the commonest being fusarium patch. It usually appears in autumn and spring and is far spreading, causing the grass to turn brown and die. The disease can be controlled by a mercury-based fungicide such as calomel and the lawn should be aerated and fed to build up its resistance. Bare patches should be pricked over and resown.

Toadstools

Toadstools often present a fairy ring, the circle of grass becoming darker than the rest of the lawn, then leaving a thin line of bare earth. The area should be spiked with a tined fork and a solution of 2 oz. of epsom salts in a gallon of water applied. If a disfiguring ring persists it may be necessary to returf, using fresh soil. Care must be taken to ensure that the infected soil is not spilled during the operation as the spores of the fungus responsible for the trouble are easily spread.

Brownish Patches

A bitch is often responsible for brownish patches that appear on the lawn. The only way of dealing with these disfiguring patches is to cut out the dead turf, and introducing fresh soil, resow.

Roses

Roses are the gardener's best investment. They are cheap, some of the best roses are still to be had for 30p; they are generous in flowering and long lived.

Soil

A good loam, the top 12 in. enriched with decayed manure or compost, suits the rose. Good drainage is important and if on heavy land, a slightly raised bed is advisable to speed up the run-away.

The Site

Borders facing south or south west do well. The bushes need plenty of air as the stagnant air of small, enclosed gardens encourages mildew, but draughts must be avoided. Roses should be kept away from big trees with their searching roots and deep shade and not planted close to hungry, greedy hedges.

When replacing a discarded bush it is important to remove the old soil and replace with fresh soil from another site.

Design and Colour Groupings

A design of different planting levels is usually more interesting than a rose garden on a flat bed. I much prefer beds of one colour, believing that flowers can easily clash with each other: orange varieties and the bicolors are better divorced from the red. The species and old roses are good mixers and seldom growl at each other.

Planting

The beds should be prepared in early September, ready for planting in the autumn. The second half of October and early November are the best times for planting before the soil has lost its summer warmth and winter frosts set in.

Should the gardener miss autumn planting he should plant at the end of March in order to avoid severe frosts. Broadly speaking, roses can be moved while they are dormant so long as the ground is not sodden or deeply frostbound.

An exception to these planting times can be made in the case of roses grown in polythene, whalehide or metal containers. These can be planted at any time of the year provided the ground is in a suitable condition to receive them. Care must be taken not to disturb the soil ball round the roots when removing them from the containers.

A rose that has a shrivelled appearance on arrival can be helped by having its roots soaked in water overnight. Unhappy plants that have been delayed in transit may be completely buried in a trench for three or four days before planting in order to recover themselves.

Bushes should be planted $1\frac{1}{2}$ to 2 ft. apart, allowing 2 ft. 6 in. between strong-growing varieties such as Peace.

The Planting Operation

Before planting, broken or damaged roots should be removed with a sharp knife or secateurs; meanwhile soft, unripe wood should be trimmed back, and long stems shortened. Dig an oblong hole to suit the plant's roots, throwing the top foot of soil to the side of the hole and replacing it with old, chopped-up turf or garden compost. This should be mixed with the lower spit of soil.

A bucketful of medium-grade neutral peat with 8 oz. of bonemeal or hoof and horn well stirred together makes a good planting mixture. Four handfuls of this should then be placed at the bottom of each hole and well worked in with the soil.

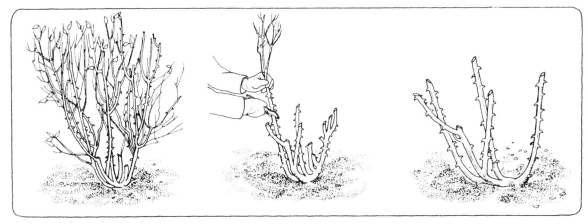

Pruning a hybrid tea rose, cutting out all dead and unwanted wood

Sit the rose on a slightly raised cushion with its crown on the mound, combing out any crossing roots with your fingers while dribbling in the planting mixture in between the roots and lightly treading it down.

The soil thrown out can now be replaced up to the soil mark on the stem of the bush which shows the depth at which the rose was previously planted. The union of stock and scion – the point where the rose variety has been budded on to the parent stock – should never be more than $\frac{1}{2}$ in. below soil level. The roots are covered with several inches of soil which should then be trodden down. Roses must be firmly planted but on heavy soil care should be taken not to compact the earth. The soil should be firmed again in the spring. Standard roses must be staked at planting time and climbers and ramblers call for the special support of trellis or wires against which they can be trained.

PRUNING

Pruning is a controversial subject but the majority of rosarians agree that mid-February in the South and late April in the North are the best times to do this work. But it should be stressed that there are those who prune success-fully in December or January.

Good pruners are vital to the job. A hooked pruning knife, the better tool, requires skill and practice and the novice is advised to start with secateurs.

A diagonal cut should be made just above the eye or dormant bud and slant away from it, great care being taken not to damage the potential shoot.

Hybrid Teas

Maiden hybrid teas (one year old) should be cut back hard immediately after planting, leaving two or three strong, stark stems of well-ripened wood with an outward point-ing eye about 3 to 4 in. above the union (marked on the stem where stock and scion meet).

After the first season moderate pruning is suggested as the general rule, allowing the plant to grow 4 to 5 in. taller every year, but each bush will call for special treatment.

Dead and diseased wood should be cut out, along with any weak, unripe twiggy stems or soft growth unlikely to survive the next frost. Crossing branches should be pruned right back and last year's growths shortened by about half their length to an outward pointing bud. The object is to create an open, cup-shaped bush which will leave the centre uncluttered and allow in plenty of light and air.

Later on as the bush matures and shows signs of losing vigour, hard pruning involving the removal of some stems to within 4 or 5 in. of the ground may be necessary to encourage basal growth.

Gardeners who inherit neglected roses should cut back one or two of the old stems to three eyes from the base and mulch the plants generously. The following year, when the plant has made some basal growth, the rest of the old wood can be removed.

In exposed gardens light autumn pruning is advisable to prevent damage from wind and root rock, and the plants should then be pruned again at the normal time.

Floribundas

By pruning young growth lightly and older growth moder-ately, dismissing old wood and encouraging new, it should be possible to keep the floribunda flowering continuously through the summer.

Ramblers and Climbers

The success of the rambler and climber depends on good pruning. The horizontal training of climbers controls the free flow of sap which encourages more blooms.

Ramblers of the Wichuraiana group such as Dorothy Perkins and Crimson Showers are treated somewhat differently. After flowering, the previous season's growth bearing the old flower trusses should be cut out at the base, and the new shoots tied in their place. Pruning is simplified by untying the rose and laying it flat on the ground.

With other ramblers which throw up only occasional basal stems, old wood high up on the plant should be cut back to the point where a young shoot is ready to take over,

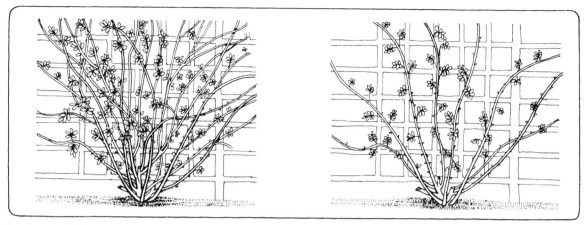

Pruning a rambler. Old stems should be removed at the base and new shoots trained in

and the shorter laterals pruned back to two or three eyes. The leading shoots are best left unpruned.

Climbing hybrid tea types are not so vigorous as their parents and pruning should be restricted to cutting out the old wood and keeping the rose within bounds. New growths should not be pruned. Much the same applies to pillar roses or moderate climbers, where all that is required is the removal of dead, or old worn-out wood. The first-year pruning should be light or omitted altogether.

Other Types
Standard roses have not the vitality of the bush rose, and severity with the knife can be dangerous; however, dead and weak wood should always be cut out. Floribunda standards can stand harder pruning and flower more effectively if cut back to main growth shoots rather than sub-laterals.

The majority of rose hedges benefit by hard pruning. Some vigorous varieties such as Queen Elizabeth, whose one fault is excessive height, need careful control, bearing in mind that very heavy pruning encourages even more vigorous growth so that a happy medium has to be achieved. Shrub roses may be left to go their own way but straggling plants can be rejuvenated by cutting out old wood stems to their base and reducing weak growth to 12 in. from the ground.

Miniature roses must be lightly dealt with, otherwise they may show their resentment by dying back.

Summing up, the aim of the rosarian when pruning should be the open, cup-shaped plant.

Propagation from Cuttings
Cuttings are an easy way of propagating roses, but, alas, they seldom possess the vigour of the budded plant and there are varieties unwilling to strike.

Those wishing to try their hand should start in August or September with a red or pink rambler or vigorous floribunda. Albertine and American Pillar will be found co-operative varieties.

Ripe shoots of early summer's growth should be chosen, and cut $\frac{1}{4}$ in. below a lower eye. The cutting should then be trimmed at the top, and reduced to 9 or 10 in. by a slanting cut made just above an eye, leaving only the two or three topmost leaves. The base of the cutting should then be dipped in a rooting hormone. A sheltered place, not overhung by trees, should be chosen and a trench of 6 to 7 in. deep dug. The bottom of the trench should be sprinkled with coarse sand.

If dry, the soil should be watered beforehand and allowed to drain away before planting. The cutting should be firmly installed with two thirds of its length underground. The protection of a frame or a cloche will increase its chances of survival. By the following spring it should be possible to see whether the cutting has rooted, indicated by the presence of new growth, and it should be ready for transplanting in the autumn.

Harden your heart and dismiss any weedy survivor; it is unlikely to make good and there are already enough hypochondriacs in most gardens.

Diseases
Mildew is a common rose disease. A spray of ordinary washing soda diluted at the rate of 1 oz. to a gallon of water will deal with a mild attack and is useful as a preventative measure. A serious infection should be sprayed with a fungicide such as dinocap.

Black spot, a destructive disease for which there is no permanent cure, can ravage a rose bed in a few days. Industrial areas are generally spared this infection being protected by sulphurous fumes.

The disease usually starts in late June, shining black dots appearing in concentric circles on the surface of the leaf. Heavily infected leaves will fall and the bush may be stripped. Any stricken leaves should be removed and burnt. The gardener should concentrate on growing healthy roses and choose the more disease-resistant varieties. Murphy's Rose Fungicide and maneb are both reliable sprays that help to control the menace.

Rust is a killer. On its appearance in early spring small sulphur-coloured swellings will be noticed on the undersurface of the leaves. The pimple-like swellings turn a bright yellow in June and then black, after which the leaf dies and falls. There is no entirely satisfactory treatment for rust. Fallen leaves must be collected and diseased stems cut out and burnt. It is wise to sacrifice and burn a single infected plant in the hope of halting an epidemic. Thiram, zineb and colloidal copper, applied from the end of May onwards, help to control the disease.

Chlorosis, causing the loss of green colouring in the leaf, denotes iron deficiency. The condition, usually appearing towards the end of spring, is prevalent on chalky soil where there is an excess of lime. Iron chelates, marketed as sequestrene, are helpful in correcting the deficiency. The gardener is advised to treat the roses affected to generous amounts of organic manure which will help to improve a chalky soil and alkaline condition.

Canker is often the result of a wound, made by blunt secateurs, through which an insect or fungus makes its entry. A browning of bark and cracks in the stem announce the infection for which there is no cure. However, the gardener can save his plant by ruthlessly pruning back to sound wood, this time, having learned his lesson, using a sharper tool.

Pests

Greenfly and blackfly belong to the sucking brigade and are best sprayed with a systemic insecticide which, taken into the sap of the plant, will protect it from the enemy for about a month.

Thrips or thunder flies, black or dark brown and about $\frac{1}{8}$ in. long, can be controlled by spraying with lindane, malathion or derris. Buds should be sprayed before they open.

The leaf-rolling sawfly is best sprayed with derris at the adult (flying) stage. The leaf-cutting bee, resembling the honey bee, which cuts out an immaculate smooth-edged circular piece of leaf or petal, is difficult to track down but a spray of derris to which a spreader (an adhesive available from the sundriesman) has been added will at least discourage her activities.

In unfavourable parts of the country, inclement weather and a severe May frost do more permanent injury to the rose than all pests and diseases put together. In a very cold area, bushes and standards may be lightly thatched with straw or bracken to protect them. Meanwhile the novice should not be discouraged; the rose has friends as well as enemies, among them the birds and the amiable ladybird.

A CHOICE OF ROSES

I present but a few from the multitude.

Hybrid Tea

The large, many-petalled flowers of splendid substance are usually carried singly or in a group of three or so on the stem. The blooms come in flushes with a resting period between the bursts, recurring intermittently throughout the summer.

Vermilion Super Star (1960) was a popular rose of the last decade, being a dramatic break in colour. Among leading hybrid teas of the day are turkey-red Ernest H. Morse; yellow Grandpa Dickson; apricot-yellow Diorama; lilac Blue Moon; bicolor Piccadilly; cream-shaded, rose-red Perfecta; and white Pascali.

Deep yellow Peace, stained cerise pink, rightly known as the rose of the century, is at times described as a little coarse, but it is a magnificent variety, particularly if only lightly pruned and allowed to become a large shrub.

I would like to recommend Pink Favourite to the novice as being disease resistant, and because I rate fragrance high I add six sweet-smelling reds to my list: deep red Josephine Bruce, Crimson Glory, Ena Harkness, Wendy Cussons, Mme Louis Laperrière, and Fragrant Cloud. Cerise Mullard Jubilee is the toast of the rosarian as I write.

Floribunda

The floribunda is the perpetual-flowering cluster rose, a non-stop blaze of colour throughout the summer and the backbone of the rose garden display.

My favourites are pure white Iceberg and clear pink Dearest, but soft pink Queen Elizabeth, Pink Parfait, salmon-pink Pernille Poulsen, the veteran non-fading Allgold and vivid red Evelyn Fison are all highly desirable. I also have a weakness for the singles, purple News and Lilac Charm.

Alas, the colourful floribundas are still, as a group, lacking in true rose scent.

Climbers

The mixed ancestry of climbers makes them difficult to classify. The repeat-flowering climbers are my first choice and among them is Golden Showers, seldom caught out of bloom during the summer months. Orange-scarlet Danse du Feu, and carmine Zéphirine Drouhin, thornless, sweet-scented and free flowering, are enchanting.

Of the climbing sports, splendid crimson Ena Harkness is famous and old-fashioned pink Mme Caroline Testout is well known for her nostalgic charm.

Among the climbing roses of the hybrid tea type pink Mme Gregoire Staechelin is richly scented and very lovely.

Ramblers and Wichuraianas

Copper-pink Albertine, single pink and white American Pillar and the old-timer, rose-pink Dorothy Perkins are never out of favour.

Climbing Species

There are a number of wild species, old and new, that climb or scramble to dizzy heights. *R. filipes* Kiftsgate from Western China, smothered in small, creamy, scented flowers of about $1\frac{1}{2}$ in. across, with winning orange stamens, is a giant climber but needs space where it can scramble and spread.

Miniatures

The miniature bushes are perfect 4- to 12-in. replicas of their large counterparts. Flame and gold Baby Masquerade is everybody's darling while tiny rose-pink Humpty Dumpty never fails to appeal. Standards and climbing miniatures are also available.

Species and Old Roses

This group has an unfailing appeal to the traditional rosarians, their one complaint being that they are rather untidy and have only one flowering period, at midsummer. Among the unforgettable are Rose of England, *Rosa alba*, the Red Rose of Lancaster, white damask Mme Hardy, *Rosa centifolia*, the cupped cabbage rosé and the exquisite moss rose.

Sheridan paid the prettiest compliment to a young woman when he invited her to 'Come into the garden. I would like my roses to see you.'

Annuals

An annual is a plant that completes its life cycle within the space of a year. Being short lived, it is in a hurry to mature, to set seed and reproduce itself. The colours are bright, hoping to attract quick fertilisation by insects near and far. Annuals are, in the main, summer plants, sown from March until June, germinating in the spring and saying goodbye in the later summer. But there are those, such as the cornflower, larkspur and marigold, which give their finest display the following year if sown in the autumn and allowed to overwinter outside. The success of autumn sowing depends much on the weather.

Placing the Annuals

Annuals are raised from seed (see Seeds, p. 20). They are essential if the border is to be kept gay from June to October and for this reason the mixed border of annuals, perennials and bedding plants is the gayest of all. A special border of annuals in the vegetable garden should be provided for the flower arranger who can then cut with a clear conscience.

I have limited my choice to 24 easy and colourful hardy annuals from an extensive list.

Alyssum (Mad Wort, Sweet Alyssum). White, pink, purple and violet. A popular edging plant. 4 to 6 in. Sow seed in April for flowering June–October, or in autumn for early flowers.

Amaranthus (Love-lies-bleeding). *Amaranthus caudatus*. Crimson or green. Drooping and sometimes furry tassels. 2½ ft. Sow April or May where plants are to flower. Summer.

Calendula (Garden or Pot Marigold). Orange, apricot, yellow and cream. Foolproof sun lover. 12 in. Sow seed in spring for June–October flowering, in autumn for early flowers.

Candytuft See Iberis

Centaurea (Cornflower, Sweet Sultan). *Centaurea cyanus*, the Cornflower. Sky and deep blue, rose and white. Single and double. 3 ft. Polka Dot dwarfs. 15 to 18 in. Sow in March or April for June–September flowering, from August–October for flowering in May.

Centaurea moschata, Sweet Sultan, Imperialis strain.

White, pink, purple, yellow. Excellent for cutting. 1½ ft. Sow in March–April or August–September. Summer.

Chrysanthemum. *Chrysanthemum carinatum* (syn. *C. tricolor*). White, daisy-like flowers, bright coloured rings at the base of the petals and purple centres. Showy. 2 ft. There is also Monarch Court Jesters, a bright strain of dwarfs, 1 to 2 ft. Sow in April, thin to 1 ft. apart. Summer.

Clarkia. White, pink and red. Hardy and unfussy. 1 ft. Sow in March or April. July–September.

Cornflower See Centaurea

Delphinium (Larkspur). White, blue, lilac, salmon-rose, scarlet. The Giant Imperial varieties are some of the best annuals we possess. Sun lovers. 3½ to 4 ft. Sow in autumn or spring where plants are to flower, as larkspurs do not transplant well. June–September.

Eschscholzia (Californian Poppy). Brilliant mixed or separate colours. Gay and easy. Semi-double, frilled and fluted flowers, open wide to the sun. 1 ft. Sow in March or April where plants are to flower and thin to 8 in. apart. June–September.

Amaranthus
(Love-lies-bleeding)

Nigella
(Love-in-a-mist)

Godetia. White, pink and red. Large flowers and generous display. Sow in March, April or September and thin severely. Seedlings do not take kindly to transplanting. July–October.

Gypsophila (Baby's Breath). White and rose pink. Chalk lover demanding well-drained soil. 12 to 18 in. Sow from March to July. Summer.

Helianthus (Sunflower). Yellow, bronze and chestnut red. Unfussy sun lover. 4 to 10 ft. Sow in April. August–October.

Iberis (Candytuft). White, pink, crimson and shades of mauve and purple. Easy and quick growing. 6 to 12 in. Sow in autumn for flowering in early summer, or spring for July–September.

Larkspur See Delphinium

Lavatera (Mallow). White and pink. Large trumpet flowers, handsome. 2 to 4 ft. Sow in spring where plants are to flower. July–September.

Limnanthes (Meadow Foam, Scrambled Egg Plant). Yellow and white. Will grow almost anywhere, resowing itself generously. 4 to 6 in. Sow in spring or autumn. May–July from autumn sowing, June to October when sown in spring.

Linum (Flax). White, blue, pink or scarlet. Succeeds on poor soil, given the sun. 1 to 2 ft. Sow March–May. July–September.

Love-in-a-mist See Nigella

Love-lies-bleeding See Amaranthus

Malcomia (Virginia Stock). White and shades of lilac, mauve red and yellow. The confetti-like flowers make this a perfect edging plant, thriving in almost any situation. 9 in. Sow in spring or September. May–September.

Mignonette See Reseda

Nasturtium See Tropaeolum

Nigella (Love-in-a-mist). Sky blue flowers amidst the lightest of feathery foliage. Sky blue Miss Jekyll is one of the belles of the family. There are also dark blue, pink and white varieties. 18 in. Sow March, April or September as thinly as possible. June–September.

Papaver (Annual Poppy). White, pink, red and delicate bicolors. Peony-flowered and Shirley strain, derived from our native field poppy. 18 to 24 in. Sow March or April where plants are to flower, as seedlings transplant badly. Shirley poppies can also be sown in September. July–September.

Phacelia. *Phacelia campanularia* is a much-loved gentian-blue dwarf. 9 in. Sow in March, April or September. June–September.

Poppy See Papaver

Reseda (Mignonette). Green tapering spikes with a dash of red. Very fragrant and pleasantly restful. 12 to 18 in. Sow April–May where plants are to flower. July–September.

Salvia (Clary). Blue, violet, pink with floral leaves or bracts that retain their colour for several months. $1\frac{1}{2}$ to 2 ft. Sow in April. July–September.

Sunflower See Helianthus

Sweet Sultan See Centaurea

Tropaeolum (Nasturtium). Golden orange, scarlet, cherry rose. The most widely grown annual, thriving on poor soil. Deadheading and constant spraying against blackfly are essential. 6 to 9 in. Sow in April–May. July–September.

Tropaeolum peregrinum (Canary Creeper). Canary yellow, elegant climber that will scale a 12-ft. trellis in one season. Sow April–May. July–September.

Virginia Stock See Malcomia

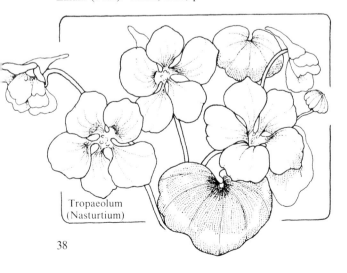

Tropaeolum
(Nasturtium)

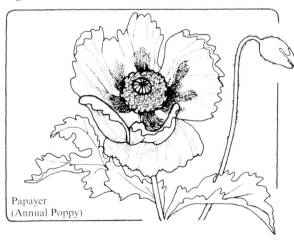

Papaver
(Annual Poppy)

Half-hardy Annuals

Half-hardy annuals require warmer conditions in the early stages than can be found in British gardens. They are usually raised from seed sown in pots or boxes in a greenhouse or frame from early February until the end of April. Many can be sown in the open ground from late May to early June, but they will flower much later.

Antirrhinum (Snapdragon). White, crimson, orange, yellow, pink; tall, intermediate and dwarf. Rust-resistant varieties should be grown where the disease is persistent. 9 in. to 3½ ft. Sow in February or March under glass or in late summer for early flowering plants. June–October.

Aster See Callistephus

Bells of Ireland See Molucella

Callistephus (China Aster). White, primrose, pink, scarlet, mauve and purple. Giants, Lilliputs and others. 9 to 15 in. Sow under glass in March or April, or in the open in late April or early May. August–September.

Carnation See Dianthus

Cineraria. *Cineraria maritima* is a useful silver foliage plant. 9 to 12 in. Summer.

Cleome (Spider Plant). Rose. Large clusters of spider-like flowers. 2 to 3 ft. Sow in March in gentle heat. Summer.

Cosmos (Cosmea). White, pink, crimson and scarlet. Single flowers on wiry stems with fern-like foliage. Easy-going sun lover. 3 to 4 ft. Sow under glass in March. July–October.

Cucurbita (Gourd). Gooseberry, teasel, fig-leaf, bottle gourd and other ornamentals. Require a sheltered position. Climbing, 3 to 4 ft. Sow under glass in gentle heat in April. June–September.

Dahlia. White, pink, red, orange, yellow and purple. Cactus flowered, single, double, dwarf bedding and pompon strains. 1½ to 3 ft. Sow at the beginning of April. Summer until frost.

Dianthus (Carnation). Chabaud mixture. White, pink, crimson, scarlet and yellow. Scented. 1½ ft. Sow February under glass or in a cold frame in spring. July–August.

Gaillardia (Blanket Flower). Crimson, orange, red and copper scarlet. Weather resistant. 15 to 18 in. Sow in March. July–September.

Gazania. Strictly a perennial, but usually treated as a half-hardy annual. Brilliant orange or orange-red daisy flowers with dark or black zones that fling themselves open to the sun. 6 to 9 in. Sow in March under glass. July–October.

Gourd See Cucurbita

Grass. Ornamental grasses, including my favourite *Briza maxima* with nodding spikelets of green and white. 1 to 2 ft. Sow in heat in March. Summer.

Ipomoea (Morning Glory). *Ipomoea tricolor* (Syn. *Pharbitis tricolor*). Blue and striped patterns, best known for variety Heavenly Blue with trumpet-shaped, azure blue flowers. One of the loveliest of all climbing plants. 10 to 15 ft. Sow under glass in March, chipping the seed or soaking it in warm water for 24 hours to help germination. Summer until autumn.

Livingstone Daisy See Mesembryanthemum

Lobelia. White, Cambridge and deep blue, sapphire, purple, and red. The trailing variety Sapphire is suitable for hanging baskets and window boxes. 6 in. Sow in warmth in February or March, or in autumn and over-winter under glass. June–October.

Marigold See Tagetes

Matthiola (Ten-week Stocks). White, primrose, lavender, pink, red and purple. 1 ft. Sow in March in gentle heat. June–July.

Ipomoea
(Morning Glory)

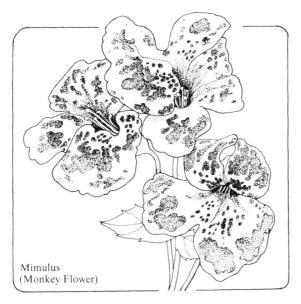

Mimulus
(Monkey Flower)

Mesembryanthemum (Livingstone Daisy). *Mesembryanthemum criniflorum*, now known as *Dorotheanthus bellidiformis*. Daisy-like flowers in dazzling colours. Thrives in dry, sunny positions and at the seaside. 3 to 4 in. Sow in a temperature of 16°C. (60°F.) in March or April. An outdoor sowing can be made in April or May for later flowering. July–September.

Mimulus (Monkey Flower). *Mimulus cupreus*. Orange, salmon or buff. Enjoys a rather moist soil. 4 ft. Sow in March. June–August.

Molucella (Bells of Ireland). The white flowers have pale, sea-green whorls delicately veined. The darling of the flower arrangers. 4 to 6 ft. Sow in late March or April in a temperature of around 16 to 18°C. (60 to 65°F.) August.

Monkey Flower See Mimulus

Morning Glory See Ipomoea

Nemesia. White, blue, primrose, red, scarlet. Requires a

Mesembryanthemum
(Livingstone Daisy)

little extra care in thinning out and hardening off. 9 to 12 in. Sow in a temperature of 16 to 18°C. (60 to 65°F.) in late March or April. July–September.

Nicotiana (Tobacco Plant). White, lime green, pink and red. The variety Lime Green is one of the best selling half-hardies. 1 to 4 ft. Sow in February or March in gentle heat. July–September.

Ornamental Cabbage and Kale. Green and purple turning to rose or pure white. Greatly favoured by the flower arranger. Enjoys a rich soil. 6 to 9 in. Sow in cold frame in January or outside in April or May. Late summer.

Ornamental Corn. Multicoloured cobs, red, yellow, orange and blue. Can be dried for winter decoration. 4 to 5 ft. Late summer.

Penstemon. A perennial treated as a half-hardy annual. White, pink, crimson trumpet-shaped blooms, some white-throated. 1½ ft. Sow in February. August until frost.

Petunia. White, mauve, purple, pink, crimson and striped. Broad, open, long, funnel-shaped flowers. Among the finest of the half-hardy border annuals but requires a good summer. 1 to 1½ ft. Sow in March. July–September.

Phlox. *Phlox drummondii*. White, pink, crimson, mauve and purple, many with contrasting eyes. 6 to 15 in. Sow under glass in early March. July–September.

Rudbeckia (Cone Flower). Golden yellow, with dark or black centres. Hybrids in yellow, brown and deep chestnut shades. Fine bicolors. 2½ to 3 ft. Sow under glass in March, or in the open ground in summer to provide early flowers the following year. July until frost.

Salpiglossis. Cream, gold and yellow, rose with gold veinings, blue, violet and purple with gold pencilling. A rich, glorious flower. 1½ to 3 ft. Sow under glass in February or March in a temperature of about 13°C. (55°F.), or outdoors in late April or early May. July–September.

Salvia. Blazing scarlet or royal purple. *S. splendens*, scarlet, and *S. patens*, a lovely blue, requiring extra care. 1 ft. Sow under glass in January or February. July–September.

Scabiosa (Pincushion Flower, Scabious). White, pink, red, pale mauve, blue, the beautiful maroon, and my favourite Black Prince. 2½ ft. Sow in April where plants are to flower or in autumn in a cold frame. July–September.

Spider Plant See Cleome

Stock See Matthiola

Tagetes (Marigold). Giant and dwarf African and dwarf French. Gold, orange, yellow, splashed with red or gold. African: 2 to 2½ ft. French: 6 to 12 in. The dwarf French varieties Spanish and Red Brocade are most rewarding. 8 to 10 in. Sow under glass in February or March or outdoors in April or May. July–September.

Verbena. White, pink, crimson, scarlet, violet-blue. Does well in wet or sunny seasons. 6 to 12 in. Sow in February under glass or outdoors in May where they are to flower. July–September.

Zinnia. White, pink, crimson, scarlet, orange or golden. Giant, Lilliput or pompon forms. 1 to 2½ ft. Sow in April under glass. May–July.

Biennials

The biennial is grown in the same way as the annual but takes two years to accomplish the cycle which the annual performs in one year. It germinates from seed in the first year and blooms the second year, after which it gives a curt farewell.

Many attractive perennials are better grown as biennials, their subsequent performance being inferior. Among these are the hollyhock, Sweet William and wallflower.

Seed may be sown on prepared seed beds during May and June but are usually sown in the late spring in boxes, pricked out when large enough to handle and planted out in the garden the second year.

I present a baker's dozen.

Althaea (Hollyhock). White, rose, pink, crimson, scarlet and yellow. Single and double, frilled and fringed. 5 to 8 ft. Sow in June or July, or treat as annuals sowing under glass in February or March. July–August.

Bellis (Double Daisy). White, pink and red. A neat edging plant. 6 in. March–June.

Campanula. *Campanula pyramidalis,* the Chimney Bell-flower. White and blue spikes, crowded with starry bells. 3 to 4 ft. July.

Canterbury Bells, *C. medium* and its varieties. Delightful white, rose-pink and blue cup-and-saucer flowers. $2\frac{1}{2}$ ft. Sow in a sunny bed in June. June–July.

Carnation See Dianthus

Cheiranthus (Wallflower). Yellow, orange, chestnut red, mauve, crimson, purple and pastel shades. With the exception of the Siberian wallflower all are deliciously scented. $1\frac{1}{2}$ ft. Sow in May and June and transplant in early autumn, moving to their flowering positions in October or November. March–May.

Dianthus (Carnation). Pink, crimson, scarlet, dwarfs and veined picotees with fringed petals. 15 in. to $2\frac{1}{2}$ ft. Sow from May to July. July–September.

Sweet William. White, pink, crimson, harlequin and auricula eyed. Lovely clustered trusses on sturdy stems. $1\frac{1}{2}$ to 2 ft. Sow in a cold frame in May, or outdoors in June or July. June.

Digitalis (Foxglove). Cream, primrose, pink and purple, spotted and blotched with maroon, some with flowers carried horizontally round the stem. 3 to 4 ft. Sow in May or June. June–July.

Forget-me-not See Myosotis

Foxglove See Digitalis

Gilia. A rich and rather rare shade of red flowers of dashing brilliance with finely cut foliage. 3 ft. Sow in May or June or treat as an annual, sowing seed in January or February, in a temperature of 16°C. (60°F.). July–September.

Hollyhock See Althaea

Lunaria (Honesty). Silver-headed, moon-shaped seed pods for drying and winter decoration. They must be cut before they have discarded their outer covering protecting them against the rain. $2\frac{1}{2}$ to 3 ft. Sow in May or June. April–May.

Matthiola (Stocks, Double Brompton). White, lavender, blue, rose and pink. A sprinkling of singles must be expected; they are the darker seedlings and can be weeded out at an early stage. 15 to 18 in. Sow in a frame in June or July. Except in mild areas they should be overwintered in a frame. March–May.

Myosotis (Forget-me-not). White, dark and light blue, pink with a yellow eye. So easily raised from seed that they are usually grown as biennials. Generously resow themselves. 6 to 12 in. Sow in May or June. March–June.

Stock See Matthiola

Sweet William See Dianthus

Wallflower See Cheiranthus

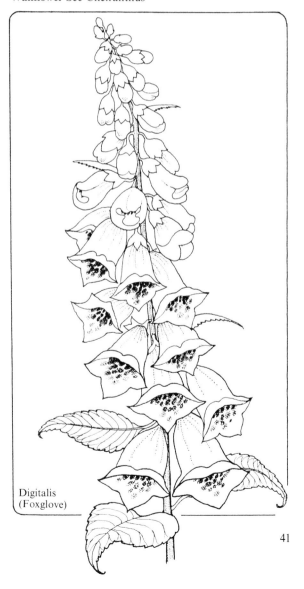

Digitalis
(Foxglove)

Bedding Plants

Bedding plants are those annually raised in pots or boxes and planted out to provide a temporary display of colour in spring or summer. They may be used to create a formal bedding scheme, or to add colour to the border, many of them making sturdy ground-cover plants. Without a greenhouse it is difficult to raise them satisfactorily, except those, such as the marigold, which are very tough.

The majority of bedding plants are annuals, but there are also useful spring biennials among them such as the wallflower, polyanthus and forget-me-not, and some perennials.

Geometrical pattern planting, floral clocks and coats of arms requiring hundreds of plants and some skill are best left to local authorities. The amateur gardener can use bedders for borders, to brighten up the front of a shrubbery, or for tubs, window boxes and hanging baskets.

The standards and taller bedders, now obtainable at garden centres, such as heliotrope, fuchsia, plumbago or one of the many varieties of *Ricinus communis* (Castor Oil Plant), growing to 5 ft. with large palmate leaves in dark crimson, purple, red or green and white, will break the line of border plants and relieve any boring flatness.

Drifts of lobelia in light and dark blue, *Phlox drummondii* or nasturtiums (with Cherry Rose to the fore) make bright ground cover and reduce weeding. I grew a packet of *Tagetes* Spanish Brocade in the kitchen last spring and carpeted a large area with the seedlings in the square where I live. They were rewarding and flowered into November.

Echeveria glauca, with coral yellow-tipped flowers, will be found a good mixer. I prefer to see this 'hen-and-chicken' subject planted in clumps and not in lines.

The petunia and zinnia are two of the most exciting and glamorous bedders we possess, provided the summer is kind. A mass planting of frilly double white petunias or the white and red ruffled veteran Cherry Tart is a happy sight. Our gardens would often be dull in June and July without these charming old favourites.

Cultivation

Soil must be well fed with rotted manure or compost before planting, after which further feeding will be unnecessary. Bedding plants should be thoroughly watered the day before they are tipped out of their pots and once planted must never be allowed to dry out. Firm planting is advised, using fingers to firm the soil round the roots rather than a trowel.

Deadheading is an important chore, not only for appearance's sake but once annuals are allowed to set seed they put all their energy into reproduction and flowering immediately slows up. The bedder has a short life and a gay one. Unless it's a perennial, once flowering is over it may be pulled up and put on the compost heap.

I have included bedding plants in the list of annuals (see p. 39) but the dahlia and the pelargonium (or geranium), two great favourites generally treated as bedders, call for fuller details of cultivation.

DAHLIA

The dahlia has succeeded in extending its flowering season and now comes into bloom in July. There are the Decoratives, Cactus, Balls, Pompons, Collerettes, Anemone centred, Fimbriated and Bedders, and new types which are described as miscellaneous.

I am accused by the growers of favouring the water-lily types classed as 'Small Decoratives', the collerettes and

Four types of dahlia

Cactus   Bedding   Pompon   Small Decorative

anemone flowered, and even the double orchid-flowering oddity Giraffe. To this I must plead guilty, for I have a weakness for the moderate-sized dahlias which are easy to handle in vases.

The dahlia is a sun lover and eats and drinks well – in fact, it is greedy. The chosen ground should be well dug in the autumn to a depth of 2 ft., and rotted manure introduced generously from the bottom of the trench upwards. If the ground is very poor, basic slag may also be added to the top spit.

It is usually safe to plant the tubers in the last week in May, but much will depend on the weather.

Strong-growing varieties should be placed 4 ft. apart, the medium 3 ft. apart, and 1 ft. should be allowed between the small bedding varieties. The tubers should be covered with 3 in. of soil and all types, other than bedders, will require staking. Should young shoots appear in a cold spell they can be protected at night by cloches or upturned flower-pots.

Once the plants are growing well, they may be treated to applications of fertiliser or liquid manure: a mulch of old manure after a fall of rain will keep the roots cool and reduce the need for watering.

Tubers should be lifted in the autumn when foliage has been blackened by frost, and labelled for identification. The stems should be cut back to 4 to 5 in. and the tubers brought inside, turned upside down to drain for a week, and the soil teased from them. They should be stored in shallow trays (not on top of each other), lightly dusted with flowers of sulphur as a precaution against disease, and covered with dry peat to prevent them shrivelling.

Dahlias should be stored in an airy, frost-proof place where the temperature does not fall below 4°C. (40°F.). The tubers must be inspected regularly during the winter and any sign of mildew wiped away with a dry cloth, then re-dusted afterwards with flowers of sulphur.

In districts where it is normally mild dahlias may be left in the ground throughout the winter, but there is always a risk that a severe frost may destroy them.

Propagation

Plants can be increased by cuttings, division of tubers or by seed.

To take cuttings, tubers are started into growth in a greenhouse or frame in February and a number of cuttings taken from the young shoots. These cuttings should be 3 in. in length and include a heel, or piece of the parent tuber. They should be dipped in a hormone rooting powder and inserted in a pot of sandy compost, later being potted up and planted out in the usual way.

To divide dahlias, the roots can be pulled apart at planting time or cut with a knife into sections. Each section should possess a shoot or portion of the old stem.

Seed is sown in pans and covered with a suspicion of sieved soil. The pans should be placed in the greenhouse and covered with glass and a sheet of brown paper. Seed will not come true from a named variety, but from some of the small bedders it will provide plants true to type which are usually pleasing. See seed sowing p. 20.

Pests and Diseases

Dahlias are persistently attacked by earwigs. The enemy can be trapped at night in upturned flower-pots filled with hay and lodged on top of stakes. The unpleasant chore of shaking the pest into a bucket of paraffin or hot water should be done next morning.

Virus disease is common among dahlias and is spread by aphids, or an infected knife, when taking cuttings. It is essential to buy good clean stock from a reputable dahlia specialist.

PELARGONIUM (GERANIUM)

This is a half-hardy plant from South Africa, the VIP of bedding plants and the pride of Queen Victoria. Though commonly known as geranium, the botanical name of this plant is pelargonium. The true geranium is a hardy perennial of the herbaceous border and quite a different genus (see p. 46).

Cultivation

Being slightly tender, pelargoniums are best planted out in early June in good fibrous loam with some peat or coarse sand added if the soil is heavy and a sprinkling of bonemeal, together with occasional feeds of well-balanced fertiliser as the plant develops. A fertiliser with a heavy nitrogen or leaf-making content should be avoided. Town gardeners growing plants in tubs and containers can use John Innes Potting Compost No. 1.

Plants should be brought indoors before any danger of frost, trimmed and potted up or boxed in wooden trays. They should be given only enough water to avoid desert dryness until the spring.

When the plants wake up in March, prune back hard and repot firmly using a tablespoonful of superphosphate of lime or a good fertiliser to each bushel. Decayed leaves must always be removed.

Propagation

Cuttings can be taken of firm shoots 3 to 4 in. long. They should be cleanly cut just below the third or fourth joint, avoiding sappy growth with large leaves. The cuttings should be dipped in hormone rooting powder after the lower leaves and stipules (small leaf appendages) have been removed. Several cuttings can then be placed around the rim of a pot filled with sandy compost. Damping off can be guarded against by giving water in the morning when the cuttings are dry. Tips of shoots may be pinched out to encourage bushiness.

As Indoor Plants

Provided the temperature does not fall below 7°C. (45°F.) the pelargonium makes a good house plant. It needs sun, light and good ventilation. Without light the leaves turn yellow through lack of chlorophyll.

Pelargonium
(Geranium)

Geranium Groups

The Regal Pelargonium. Statelier and grander than the zonal pelargonium, this plant can be grown outdoors in summer, but is looked upon mainly as a greenhouse plant as it is vulnerable to rain and weather.

The famous Victorian Carisbrooke, soft rose pink with maroon markings, is a beauty.

The Zonal Pelargonium. This is the plant known to everyone as 'geranium', with leaves marked with a zone or band.

Here Gustav Emich, the semi-double known as 'The Buckingham Palace Geranium', has ousted the veteran Paul Crampel, being more weather and wind resistant. Festiva Maxima, purple double; Decorator, semi-double crimson-scarlet; King of Denmark, salmon-pink and his slightly darker Queen, and Heroine, the best double white for bedding, still hold their place.

The Irene strain of pelargoniums introduced during the last few years have proved themselves healthy, early and free flowering. Irene, a good pink, leads the group and is particularly useful for tubs and courtyards.

The Scented-leaved Pelargonium. This is grown for its fragrant foliage. There are lemon, orange and mint-scented varieties: *Pelargonium tomentosum,* peppermint scented with flat, hairy leaves and low spreading growth, makes an excellent house plant.

The Variegated-leaved Pelargonium. Mrs Henry Cox, the brightest tricolor, gold-bronze, red and cream, must surely head the list.

The Ivy-leaved Pelargonium. The pelargonium specialist can provide an exciting list of these lovely plants. My favourite La France, semi-double lilac with maroon markings on the upper petals, and mauve and pink Galilee should not be missed, while perhaps the most famous of all Victorians, L'Elégante, with variegated cream and purple scented leaves and insignificant white flowers, is still a popular house or porch plant.

The Miniature Pelargonium. This plant rarely exceeds 8 to 9 in. and, like its larger counterparts, demands the sun. Black Vesuvius with single salmon flowers is an outstanding veteran. Best grown in $2\frac{1}{2}$- to 3-in. pots, the miniatures should never be allowed to dry out.

Perennials

Perennial plants flower each year and live for an indefinite period.

Many plants can be raised quite easily from outdoor sowings made in late spring and summer, with or without glass protection.

A host of gay plants such as aubrieta, delphinium, lupin or pinks can be raised from a packet of seed. The seed packet is a boon to the novice with a new and empty garden even if the resulting plants are not as exciting as the latest named varieties, which can only be obtained from cuttings or division.

The perennial is the permanent resident in the herbaceous border. Every year a third of the border should be dug over and fed with humus-forming material such as compost or manure, and the plants divided. Exceptions to this rule are the peonies and a few others that resent disturbance. A dressing of bonemeal in spring followed by a feed of general fertiliser applied at 2 to 3 oz. per square yard during the growing season will keep the plants in good order.

In the South, the herbaceous plants may be cut down to the ground when they have died back in late autumn, but in the North and in cold districts the dead stems may be left until the spring as they will help protect the roots against frost and cold.

In giving my recommendations for the basis of the herbaceous border, let me say now, to save repetition, that all the following subjects need good, well-drained soil and an open, sunny position, unless otherwise stated.

Acanthus (Bear's Breeches). Dull pink or white, suffused rose. Stiff spikes and large classical leaves. 3 to 4 ft. Summer. Propagation: seed or division in spring.

Achillea (Milfoil, Yarrow). Flat-headed yellow flowers on stiff silvery stems with an attraction for the butterfly. 4 ft. and over. July–August. Dried heads will last the winter through. Superior varieties only should be grown. Propagation: division in spring or autumn; cuttings can also be taken in early summer.

Allium. There are 280 species of garlic. Ornamental species have blue, purple, lilac and rose-pink flowers. 1 to 2 ft. July–August. Propagation: seed in March; offsets and bulbils in autumn or spring.

Alstroemeria (Peruvian Lily). Orange trumpet flowers. Pink to flame Ligtu Hybrids are an improved form, though not easy customers to establish. 3 to 4 ft. June–July. When buying, pot-grown plants are advised, in order to avoid root disturbance. Propagation: seeds sown in spring in small peat pots, one to each pot; division in spring or autumn.

Alyssum (Madwort, Gold Dust). Yellow or golden showy flowers. Easy to grow, but requires firm pruning. 6 to 9 in. May–June. Propagation: seed sown in frames in March or outdoors in April; half-ripe cuttings rooted in a frame in early summer.

Anchusa (Borage). Light to deep blue. 3 to 6 ft. June–August. Propagation: a challenge, but young stock is essential. Seed sown in March: seedlings often variable; also root cuttings inserted in sandy soil in winter.

Anemone (Windflower). White, rose to red. Important late summer or autumn flower. Unfussy once established and suitable for semi-shade. $2\frac{1}{2}$ ft. Propagation: seed sown in sandy soil in a frame in spring; division after flowering; root cuttings in autumn or spring.

Aquilegia (Columbine). Slender white, blue and crimson flowers, graceful and spurred. Tolerates partial shade. $1\frac{1}{2}$ to 3 ft. May–June. Propagation: seed sown in a frame in August or semi-shaded bed in May or June. Often self-sown. High percentage of rogues–untrue to parents–is usual.

Aster (Michaelmas Daisy). Over a hundred named varieties in blue, purple, pink and white. Backbone of autumn border. Enjoys well-rotted manure. Vulnerable to mildew; annual division helps to lessen the problem but a preventive spray is essential. The plant is best restricted to four or five stems only. $2\frac{1}{2}$ to 5 ft. Late summer to autumn. Propagation: division in spring or autumn; softwood cuttings rooted in sandy soil in a shaded frame March–June.

Campanula (Bellflower). Vast family. Blue, white and pink. Named varieties are recommended. 1 to 4 or 5 ft. June–September. Propagation: seed; division of roots in spring or autumn; softwood cuttings in March.

Catananche. A semi-everlasting cornflower-type perennial with a zest for flowering. 2 to $2\frac{1}{2}$ ft. June–August. Propagation: seed in early spring; root cuttings in autumn; division in spring.

Centaurea. Cornflower-shaped flowers. Silvery foliage. *Centaurea dealbata* pink-magenta. 2 to 3 ft. July–August. Propagation: division every two or three years in spring or autumn.

Chrysanthemum. *Chrysanthemum maximum,* the white Shasta Daisy. Korean and Rubellum, important autumn border plants. White, pink, red, yellow, orange and bronze. No disbudding and little staking necessary but they require sunshine and good fare. $2\frac{1}{2}$ to 3 ft. August until frost. Propagation: division in autumn or spring. *C. maximum* varieties by softwood cuttings in mid-summer.

Aquilegia
(Columbine)

Dahlia See p. 42

Delphinium. Plant of regal beauty. White, sky to gentian blue, pink, purple and now reds are on their way. Impressive spikes of bloom 3 to 7 ft. June–July. Propagation: seeds sown under glass in March or outdoors in April; root cuttings, spring stem cuttings; division in autumn or spring.

Dianthus. The much-loved garden pinks and the border carnations in many colours. Enchanting pink Doris, and Dad's Favourite, double white with chocolate markings, must not be missed. 9 in. Summer. Propagation: seed in spring; cuttings from non-flowering shoots in a cold frame in summer.

Dicentra (Dutchman's Breeches, Bleeding Heart). Pink and white with lovely arching stems. Liable to die out if not given semi-shade and moisture. Should be treated to peat dressings. 1 to $1\frac{1}{2}$ ft. May–June. Propagation: division from October onwards or in early spring.

Doronicum (Leopard's Bane). Golden yellow. Harpur

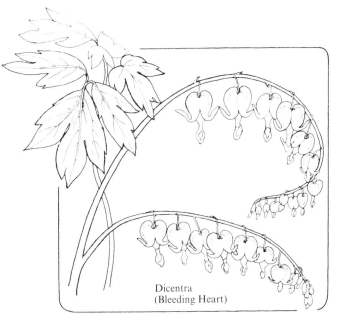

Dicentra
(Bleeding Heart)

Crew an outstanding variety. Often the first herbaceous plant to flower in the spring. 2 to 2½ ft. April–May. Propagation: division in spring or autumn.

Echinops (Globe Thistle). Blue. Requires deep cultivated soil. Dislikes disturbance. 3 to 4 ft. Summer. Propagation: seeds sown outdoors in April; division between October and March; root cuttings taken in late autumn or winter and raised in a cold frame.

Erigeron (Fleabane). Pink and lilac-blue daisy flowers. Thrives in moist borders. 2 to 2½ ft. Long flowering. Summer. Propagation: division in October or March.

Eryngium (Sea Holly). Steel-blue and violet flowers and spiny-toothed leaves. 2 to 2½ ft. July–August. Propagation: seed sown in a cold frame in April or May; division in October or April; root cuttings in autumn or winter in a cold frame.

Euphorbia (Spurge). Inconspicuous flowers; the yellow-

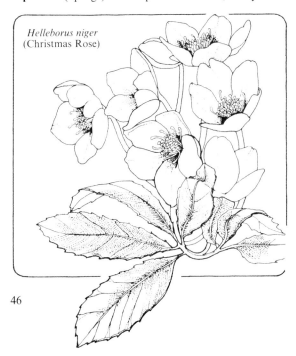

Helleborus niger
(Christmas Rose)

green foliage-like bracts are appreciated by flower arrangers. Enjoys a rather dry position. 1 to 3 ft. Spring. Propagation: seed in April; cuttings in a cold frame in sandy soil, summer; division in October or April.

Gaillardia. Yellow, bronze and red. Must be given a well-drained position. Light soil and sun. Plant in spring. Mulch with decayed manure in summer. 2 to 3 ft. July to August. Propagation: division in spring.

Geranium (Cranes-bill). The hardy geraniums are easy to grow in any good soil, in full sun or semi-shade. They make excellent ground cover, their luxuriant growth being impenetrable by weeds.

Geranium endressii has bright pink flowers but *G. pratense,* the blue geranium with saucer-shaped flowers in June and July, height 2 ft., is for me the pick of the family. Propagation: seed under glass in early March or outdoors in late March or April; root division in spring and autumn.

Geum. Red and yellow. Enjoys rather poor soil, particularly in winter. 2 ft. Summer. Propagation: seed in a cool greenhouse or frame in March; division in spring or autumn.

Gypsophila (Chalk Plant). White and pale pink fairy-like flowers. Has a liking for chalk and mortar rubble. 2 to 3 ft. June–August. Propagation: not easy, but robust basal side shoots with a heel taken in summer might be tried.

Helenium. Daisy flowers in yellow, bronze, mahogany and nut red. Easy if not overbaked by the sun. Propagation: seed sown in a cool greenhouse in spring; division in autumn or spring.

Helianthus (Sunflower). Yellow. One of the tallest herbaceous plants. Roots invasive and should be controlled. Immense flowers if disbudded. 5 to 7 ft. August–early October. Propagation: seed sown outdoors in April; division in spring or autumn. (See also Annuals p. 38.)

Helichrysum (Everlasting Flower). There are only a few perennial species of this genus. 6 in. to 3½ ft. May–August. Propagation: seed sown out of doors in April; cuttings rooted in a cold frame in spring; shrubby species by half-ripened wood in a cold frame in summer.

Helleborus. *Helleborus niger,* the Christmas Rose. White, rose, green. White variety should be covered with a cloche to protect the petals. Thrives on rich loam in semi-shade. Mulch with manure in spring. Water freely in dry weather. Dislikes disturbance. 1 to 2 ft. February–April. Propagation: seeds sown in sandy soil in a cold frame in October or March; division of roots in March.

Hemerocallis (Day Lily). Many new American hybrids, yellow, orange, pink and red. Flowers last one day only, but are quickly followed by others. Mulch with manure in spring. 2 to 3 ft. June–July. Propagation: division in October or March.

Heuchera (Coral Flower). A much improved genus with graceful sprays of pink, copper, crimson flowers. Dislikes heavy soil or wet clay. 1½ to 2 ft. Summer. Propagation: seed sown in light soil in a cold frame in spring; division in spring.

Heucherella. A cross between *Heuchera* and *Tiarella;* flowers not unlike heuchera in charming shades of pink.

1 ft. May–June. Propagation: division in autumn or spring.

Hosta (Plantain Lily, Funkia). Fashionable foliage and ground-cover plant with unimportant lilac flowers. An annual dressing of rotted manure is appreciated. Useful for growing in shade or a north aspect. 2 to 2½ ft. July. Propagation: division in autumn or spring.

Incarvillea (Chinese Trumpet Flower). Rosy magenta. Needs sheltered position and light winter protection of straw or bracken in cold gardens. 6 in. to 2 ft. Summer. Propagation: seed sown in a cold frame in March; division in spring.

Inula. Yellow daisy-like flower. Unfussy provided the soil is not too arid. 2 to 3 ft. June–August. Propagation: seed is likely to be variable; division in autumn or spring.

Iris. Tall bearded and dwarf, in glorious colours. Short flowering period. Enjoys mortar rubble, and taste of lime. Good drainage and sunshine essential. Rhizomes must be kept near the surface to bake in the sun. 2 to 3½ ft. May–June. Propagation: division of rhizomes immediately after flowering.

Kentranthus (Red Valerian). Rosy pink. Trouble free; excellent on chalk or dry wall. 2 to 3 ft. June–July. Propagation: easily raised from seed sown in a frame or greenhouse in March, or from cuttings.

Kniphofia (Red-hot Poker). Scarlet, orange, yellow and white varieties. Dislikes cold, wet soil. Grass-like foliage may be tied round crown for winter protection. 2 to 5 ft. July–August. Propagation: seed, or division in autumn or spring.

Liatris (Kansas Gay Feather, Button Snakeroot). Reddish-purple straight spikes of flowers opening from the top downwards, contrary to usual practice. 3 to 3½ ft. Summer and autumn. Propagation: division of the tuberous roots in spring.

Lobelia. *Lobelia cardinalis*, with striking scarlet flowers and purple foliage, is a favourite plant of mine. Hardy only in warm gardens in the South. 3 to 4 ft. Propagation: division in spring.

Limonium (Statice, Sea Lavender). An everlasting flower used for winter decoration. Lavender blue. 3 ft. August. Propagation: seed sown outdoors in spring, but winter root cuttings are more reliable.

Lupinus (Lupin). Russell's hybrids possess a wonderful range of colour, though they have not quite the stamina of their forerunners. Fortunately the plant flowers as a yearling. Old plants resent disturbance. The rumour that lupins revert to blue is unfounded, but self-sown seedlings oust the more delicate hybrids. Enjoys sandy loam and a little shade. 2½ to 3 ft. June–July. Propagation: seed sown outdoors in April; cuttings in March (solid, not hollow shoots) rooted in sandy soil in a cold frame.

Lychnis (Campion). Vivid scarlet or white. 3 ft. June–August. Propagation: seed sown outdoors in March or April; division in spring or October.

Lysimachia (Loosestrife). Excellent genus for damp places. Yellow or white flowers. 3 ft. The beloved yellow Creeping Jenny belongs to this family. 1 in. June–September.

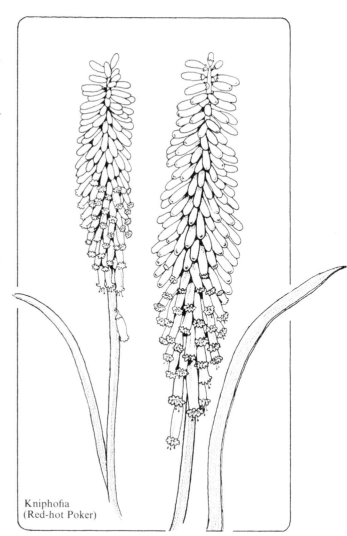

Kniphofia
(Red-hot Poker)

Propagation: seed or division in the autumn or spring.

Meconopsis. *Meconopsis cambrica*, the yellow Welsh Poppy. Grey-green foliage. 1 to 1½ ft. May–August. Propagation: seed saved from the best plants.

M. betonicifolia, the Himalayan Blue Poppy, still known by many as *M. baileyi*, is the star turn. By no means easy, it is vulnerable to damp and must not be allowed to flower the first year. Happier given shade and prefers peat and leafmould to lime. 3 to 5 ft. June–July. Propagation: seed sown in sandy peat in a cold frame in spring. Seedlings are variable in colour and the gardener should discard inferior blue-purples.

Michaelmas Daisy See Aster

Mimulus (Musk, Monkey Flower). A moisture lover in yellow, tangerine, crimson and cerise. Unfortunately this gay little flower has lost its scent. 1 to 4 ft. May–August. Propagation: seed or cuttings in spring or summer.

Monarda (Bergamot). Red and pink, with nettle-like aromatic foliage. A useful plant providing colour in late summer. June–September. Propagation: division in autumn or spring.

Nepeta (Catmint). Lavender blue with grey foliage. A sun lover, and useful edging plant, thriving in light soil. 1½ to 2 ft. June–September. Propagation: young growths rooted in a cold frame in sandy soil in summer; division in March.

Obedient Plant See Physostegia

Oenothera (Evening Primrose). Yellow. Enjoys light soil and sunshine. 1½ to 2 ft. July–August. Propagation: seed sown in a cold frame in March or April; cuttings taken in spring and rooted in sandy soil in a frame; division in early spring.

Paeonia (Peony). Pink, white, red and yellow, single and double. Hardy as a polar bear and likely to outlive the planter. Dislikes disturbance. Deep planting should be avoided as it results in absence of bloom. The crown should be lifted if it sinks lower than 2 in. below the soil surface. A gross feeder that responds to a mulch of stable manure in February, and an autumn dressing of bonemeal. 2 to 3 ft. May–June. Propagation: division in early spring. Species can be increased by seed sown in boxes or pots in sandy soil in September and placed in a frame.

Papaver. *Papaver orientale,* the Oriental Poppy, is a noble flower with grand varieties in scarlet, crimson, orange, salmon pink and white. Foliage likely to become untidy. 2½ ft. May–June. Propagation: seed sown outdoors in May–June; root cuttings 2 in. long taken in April or when lifting in autumn and rooted in gritty compost in a cold frame.

Pelargonium (Geranium). See p. 43.

Phlox. All colours other than true blue and yellow. Responds to good fare and moisture-retentive soil. Requires regular soakings during drought. Semi-shaded position preferred. Vulnerable to eelworm. 2½ to 3½ ft. July–August. Propagation: division in October or March; root cuttings taken early and rooted in a cold frame in February or March.

Paeonia
(Peony)

Physostegia (Obedient Plant). Rose, white. 1 to 1½ ft. September. Propagation: division in spring.

Platycodon (Chinese Bellflower, Balloon Flower). A relation of the campanula. Deep blue, white. 1 to 2 ft. August–September. Propagation: seed sown under glass in a temperature of 13°C. (55°F.) in March or August; division in spring.

Primula. Immense race embracing auricula, cowslip, primrose and polyanthus, revelling in light shade and moisture. 6 to 12 in. March–May. Propagation: seed; division.

Pyrethrum. Member of the chrysanthemum family. Single and double daisy-like flowers. Temperamental and unhappy in heavy soil. Best planted in spring. 2 to 2½ ft. May–June. Propagation: seed; careful division after flowering.

Ranunculus. A buttercup flower in a splendid range of colours. Moist, shady position essential. 2 ft. Spring. Propagation: seed sown as soon as ripe in a cold frame; division in spring or October.

Red-hot Poker See Kniphofia

Romneya (Californian Tree Poppy). Immense white poppy-like flowers with telling golden stamens and blue-grey foliage. *Romneya coulteri* is a sun lover content with poorish stony soil provided it is well drained. Slow to settle down but once established it increases fast by underground runners. A superb perennial. Propagation: seed sown in a greenhouse in temperature of 13°C. (55°F.) in spring; root cuttings in spring.

Rudbeckia (Cone Flower). A tall yellow black- or orange-eyed flower happy in ordinary dryish soil if given a mulch of manure in the spring, and a fine summer. 3 to 5 ft. June–November. Propagation: seed sown outdoors in March or April; division in autumn or spring.

Salvia (Sage). The blue-purple perennial salvia is an excellent border plant. Lovely *Salvia turkestanica,* the Vatican sage, with hooded blooms decorated with rosy-lavender bracts is safer treated as a biennial. 1½ to 5 ft. June–November. Propagation: division in spring or autumn.

Saxifraga See p. 50

Scabiosa (Scabious, Pincushion Flower). Mauve Clive Greaves is the most successful cut flower but it cannot survive in wet soil. Best planted in spring. 1½ to 2 ft. Summer. Propagation: seeds sown in spring under glass; division in spring; cuttings with a basal heel inserted in a frame or greenhouse in spring.

Sedum (Stonecrop). Succulent. *Sedum spectabile,* pink and red with glaucous foliage and floral platters that have a fascination for the Tortoiseshell and Red Admiral butterflies. William Robinson, the landscape gardener, referred to the sedums as the 'Everlasting live-longs'. A family suited to the rock garden. 6 in. to 2 ft. July–October. Propagation: division in spring or autumn.

Sempervivum See p. 50

Sidalcea. Slender spikes of pink and crimson flowers. 2 to 5 ft. August. Propagation: division in spring or autumn.

Solidago (Golden or Aaron's Rod). Easy-going, rather

coarse plant with small, daisy-like yellow flowers. 2 to 5 ft. August–September. Propagation: division in autumn or spring.

Stachys (Betony, Lamb's Ears). *Stachys lanata* has remarkably soft and silky grey leaves. The red-purple flowers and stems are dressed in grey down. A lovable, indestructible subject that does well in the poorest of soils. 1 to 1½ ft. July. Propagation: division at any time of the year.

Thalictrum (Meadow Rue). An entrancing plant with tiny fairy-like lilac and yellow flowers and foliage as finely cut as Maidenhair fern. Dislikes disturbance. 2 to 5 ft. June–August. Propagation: seed or division in early spring.

Thymus See p. 52

Tradescantia (Spiderwort). Three-petalled violet-purple flowers; a dependable performer. 2 ft. June–September. Propagation: seed is rare; division in spring.

Trollius (Globe Flower). Round, yellow or golden buttercup flowers. Enjoys moist soil. 1½ to 2 ft. May–June. Propagation: seed sown outdoors in shade in April or September; division in autumn or spring.

Verbascum (Mullein). Tapering spikes of yellow, apricot, buff or pink blooms with silvery foliage. 3 to 6 ft. June–September. Propagation: root cuttings 3 to 4 in. long taken in autumn or winter and lightly covered with sandy compost; division or seed in spring.

The Rock Garden

Rock gardening is the specialist's game, and appeals to those who like the pigmy shrubs, miniature plants and ground creepers. A well-drained, sheltered open site should be chosen for the rock plants, many of them mountain alpines that love the sun.

The garden is best built on a slope, using sandstone, limestone or any good looking local stone. Tufa, a stone which readily absorbs and holds moisture, suits lime lovers, but is unfortunately pecked at unmercifully by pigeons, while concrete gives the rock garden a suburban air, and is unsympathetic to plants.

The rocks should be set in the soil at a slight backward-sloping angle and embedded by at least one third to resemble as near as possible a natural outcrop. It is better to use a few good-sized rocks well placed than several small ones scattered at random over the surface. Flat pockets of soil should be provided between the rocks and in crevices for planting.

Soil

Many alpines prefer a slightly acid soil. A good loam with a generous addition of peat and leafmould, plus grit and soft sand suits most of them. Pep-up, quick-acting fertilisers are not advised but a hungry plant may be treated to a sprinkling of hoof and horn meal from time to time.

Lime lovers can be given limestone chips and mortar rubble, and other favourites a special diet, once they are settled in their individual pockets.

The Alpine Meadow

Rocks and crevices are not a necessity to alpines, and the alpine meadow carpeted with creeping ground huggers has tremendous charm. True, it will not provide the cool root-run demanded by thrift and thyme and some of the mountain lovers, but a regiment of rock plants will join in the meadow tapestry along with a host of small bulbs.

Cultivation

Weeding must be regular and intensive, root and all. The watering can should be fitted with a rose so that the soil is not washed away from the plant roots. Fallen leaves must be removed and faded flowers cut off with light shears or scissors. Winter protection may be given to treasured favourites by placing a sheet of glass supported by pegs above the plants.

Rock plants are usually sold in pots and although they can be put in at any time, on heavy soil they are best planted in the spring. A small collection from an alpine specialist makes a good beginning.

THE DRY WALL

A dry stone wall is helpful in holding back soil that has been excavated when terraces of different heights have been landscaped, but it cannot be expected to buttress great weights. It can be made of bricks, York or Somerset walling stone. A layer of soil is laid between the stones in place of mortar or cement but the bricks should be bonded or staggered in the ordinary way.

It is advisable to build the wall on a stone foundation and to give it a slight backward tilt: the wall may be topped with a flat coping stone, or aubrieta or rock garden plants can be planted to trail over the edge.

House leeks, sedums and other rock plants that enjoy dryness will revel in the spaces that present themselves in the face of the wall. To avoid damaging the roots, it is best to plant them in the soil pockets between the stones while the wall is being built.

SUGGESTED PLANTS FOR THE ROCK GARDEN

Achillea (Yarrow). Gold and yellow flower clusters and thick, silvery growth. 6 in. May–June.

Ajuga (Bugle). *Ajuga reptans* is a tough plant with flowers

Planting in the pockets of soil between the stones while constructing a dry stone wall

in shades of blue. Variegated foliage, 6 in. May–June.

Alyssum. *Alyssum saxatile.* Yellow or gold with grey foliage. 6 in. April–June.

Arabis (Rock Cress). Pink or white Rosabella is a charmer. 5 in. Early spring.

Armeria (Thrift). Pink, red or white. Cushion-forming foliage. 4 to 6 in. May–June.

Aubrieta. Pink, mauve, purple, crimson, lilac flowers and shades between. Trailing foliage. March–June.

Campanula (Bellflower). Plants 3 to 12 in. tall of prostrate habit. *Campanula portenschlagiana,* with a host of open bright blue flower clusters, is a delight. 4 in. June–July.

Dianthus. A profusion of red and pink flowers on spiky grey-blue foliage. Lime lovers. Mars is a deep red double. 6 in. Summer.

Dryas. *Dryas octopetala* forms mats of dark green foliage with large white flowers and golden stamens. 3 to 5 in. May–June.

Erica (Heather). *Erica carnea.* Crimson. A gay little plant that should not be missed. 6 to 9 in. Winter.

Gentiana. *Gentiana acaulis* has glorious deep blue trumpet flowers. 3 to 4 in. April–June. *G. sino-ornata* is bright blue. 4 in. August–November.

Helianthemum (Sun Rose). Evergreen shrub in white, pink, crimson, yellow, orange and bronze. Spreads rapidly in light sandy soil. Low growing. Summer.

Iberis. *Iberis sempervirens,* evergreen candytuft. White. Undemanding. 8 to 10 in. April–June.

Leontopodium (Alpine Edelweiss). Unfortunately the woolly foliage and flowers are often more grey than white. Temperamental. 6 in. June–July.

Lewisia. Hybrid strain, pink to crimson; free-flowering lime haters. 12 in. May–June.

Lithospermum. A slightly tender evergreen with superb gentian-blue flowers. Heavenly Blue is a gem for a warm, lime-free soil. 5 to 6 in. Summer.

Mimulus (Musk). Red-brown, yellow and scarlet flowers,

a lover of cool, moist situations. 3 to 4 in. Early summer.

Phlox. *Phlox douglasii,* white; *P.:d.* Boothman's Variety, hummocks starred with clear mauve flowers, and Rosea, silvery pink. All 2 in. Splendid spring carpeters. *P. subulata,* white, pink, mauve or carmine. 4 in. May–June.

Potentilla. *Potentilla aurea plena.* Tufts of glossy leaves and double yellow flowers. 3 in. June–July.

Pulsatilla. *Pulsatilla vulgaris,* the Pasque flower, purple-violet, golden stamens, silky stems. Sun and lime lover. 12 in. Spring.

Primula. *Primula auricula,* Dusty Miller, *P. denticulata,* the drumstick primula, *P. juliae* magenta, *P. marginata,* lavender blue and others of the family should be considered. 12 in. March–May.

Ramonda. *Ramonda myconi,* violet flowers. The plants should be placed in clumps with small ferns as their neighbours. 4 in. June.

Rosa. The dwarf rose is the perfect miniature in every way. Tiny bushes 4 to 12 in. high. Summer.

Saxifraga. Silver-edged foliage, silver and green hummocks and large or small rosettes with white, pink, crimson or yellow flowers. This important family includes the cushion saxifrage or Kabschias; the encrusted and mossy types and *Saxifraga umbrosa,* the one and only London Pride. 2 to 12 in. March–July.

Sedum (Stonecrop). Another large genus with succulent leaves and pink, red, purple, or yellow flowers. An ardent sun lover. 3 to 6 in. June–October.

Sempervivum (Houseleek). Fleshy rosettes, some meticulously cobwebbed. Hard to kill; easy to increase. 2 to 12 in. Mainly summer.

The rich purple and yellow of aubrieta and alyssum provide a cascade of colour against the mellow background of a stone wall. These plants, with their trailing habit, are well suited for planting in the crevices between the stones

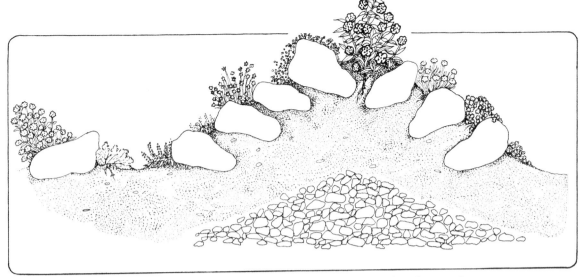

Profile of a rock garden. Notice the backward-sloping angle at which the rocks are set into the ground

Thymus (Thyme). Green, yellow or silver fragrant foliage with white or purple flowers. 1 to 8 in. June–August.

Viola. Violet: sweet scented, blue and white. Pansy: the horned violet makes a pleasant mat smothered with dark violet flowers. 8 to 10 in. May–August.

BULBS FOR THE ROCK GARDEN

The crevices and small pockets in the rock garden are ideal for miniature bulbs.

Anemone. *Anemone blanda,* deep blue, St Brigid or de Caen in many rich colours. 6 in. January–March.

Chionodoxa (Glory of the Snow). Blue and white. 6 in. March.

Crocus. Species, Dutch and Autumn-flowering Crocus.

Eranthis (Winter Aconite). Yellow, 2 to 4 in. January–March.

Erythronium. *Erythronium dens-canis,* Dog's-tooth Violet, rose. 6 in. Spring.

Fritillaria. *Fritillaria meleagris,* the Snake's Head Fritillary, drooping, lamp-like flower in purple, yellow and white. 12 to 18 in. May.

Galanthus (Snowdrop). Single and double. White. 6 in. January–March.

Hyacinthus. *Hyacinthus amethystinus, H. azureus* and *H. dalmaticus.* The elegant Alpine hyacinths, blue. 6 to 8 in. Spring.

Iris. Bulbous-rooted perennials. *Iris reticulata,* violet-purple, 6 to 8 in., dwarf *I. histrioides* Major, bright blue, 3 to 4 in. and *I. danfordiae,* canary yellow, 4 in. January–March.

Leucojum (Snowflake). White and green. 1 ft. May.

Narcissus (Daffodil). *Narcissus bulbocodium,* yellow, 6 in., and other miniatures.

Muscari (Grape Hyacinth). Deep blue, 6 in. Spring.

Ornithogalum (Star of Bethlehem). *Ornithogalum umbellatum,* white, 1 ft. May.

Puschkinia (Striped Squill). White, striped with blue. 4 in. Spring.

Scilla (Endymion). Squill. Blue, pink and white forms. 4 to 6 in. Spring.

Sparaxis (Harlequin Flower). Rather tender, requiring a warm position. Brilliant colour combinations. 6 to 8 in. May.

Tulip. *Tulipa kaufmanniana,* Water-lily Tulip. A batch of these and other taller species will give a splash of exciting colour. 6 in. March.

The Garden Pool

Pools are fashionable, and many gardeners are alive to the fascination of water in the garden, both the look and the sound of it.

Concrete is still the best material to use for lasting results, provided the owner is not afraid of the hard work involved and is careful to paint the final surface with a good water-proofing compound. The concrete must be of the best quality, laid in one operation and allowed to harden properly before the pool is filled. It should be protected in summer while hardening off with damp sacking, to prevent it drying too quickly and cracking in the sun.

Glassfibre and plastic prefabricated pools are easily

Diagram of a water garden, showing the relative positions of rock, waterside, marginal and pool plants

installed, but must be firmly seated. If polythene sheeting is used it should be of heavy duty, 500 gauge, and the pool always kept well filled with water, since the sun's rays will weaken the strength of any exposed material.

The site should be in full sun. Overhanging trees, although romantic looking, cast shade and their falling leaves cause pollution.

Small mechanical pumps can be installed for working fountains, cascades and waterfalls; this work should be done by an experienced electrician. For those who find a fountain too disturbing, there is the gurgling mill-wheel, with the water running up through the centre, and, after flooding and fanning over the surface, tumbling down to a pebbled pool.

Construction

Preparation and depth of the pool will depend on the plants to be grown. Water lilies will thrive in a depth of 18 in. of water, whereas marginal plants require only 3 to 4 in. When preparing a concrete pool, allowance must be made for a 6-in. layer of concrete and a 6-in. bed of compost, so that excavation should be made to a depth of 2 ft. 6 in. at the deepest part. A shelf or ledge at a shallower level – a 10-in. excavation allows for 4 in. of concrete, 3 in. of compost and 3 in. of water – will give an area for growing marginal plants.

When excavating the cavity for a plastic pool make sure the surface is free of stones and debris which might puncture the fabric, and that there are no hollows so that the glassfibre shell fits levelly and snugly on the soil.

Pools with a polythene or PVC liner are the cheapest and simplest to construct, but are the least durable. It is particularly important to provide a smooth base, excavating to a depth of 20 to 24 in. to allow for a 6-in. bed of compost, and removing all stones and sharp flints. A 1-in. layer of sand will help protect the sheeting from any sharp objects that have been overlooked. The sheeting is held in place by heavy stones round the edge while the pool is being filled, and afterwards the edges can be trimmed and concealed by paving slabs, or turf which gives a more naturalistic effect.

If a pool is constructed on a terrace, it should have some form of coping or demarcation built round it for safety's sake. There are prefabricated designs that provide planting holes for kingcups, iris or arum lilies which are helpful in softening the lines of the edge of the pool.

Planting

There are two methods of planting: either directly into a bed of soil 5 to 6 in. deep covering the bottom of the pool, or planting in plastic, wooden or wire-mesh baskets in which the soil is contained. The ideal soil is a heavy, rich loam with the addition of coarse bonemeal at the rate of 2 oz. to a 2-gallon bucket of soil. Bulk organic manures should not be added as they cause fermentation. A 1-in. layer of sand or shingle will help keep the soil in place.

Plants should be introduced from March to July. If rainwater is available it will be found kinder both to fish and plants than hard tap water. Neither plant life nor fish will prosper in a pool with a forceful fountain in the middle.

It is better to fill the pool gradually, adding more water at intervals as the plants grow, until the full depth is reached after three or four weeks. There may be some cloudiness at first due to chemical changes in the water, but this will eventually clear.

If fish are to be added to the pool some oxygenating plants will be needed to keep the water clean and give them some shelter. These free-floating plants are simply dropped into the water without any soil. Fish should not be introduced for the first few weeks until the plants have become established and the water has cleared.

Water Lilies

The water lily with its immaculate flowers and flat, floating pads, has pride of place. It can be planted in a basket, or in a heavy loam bed at the bottom of the pool at depths varying from 10 to 24 in., depending on variety.

Care must be taken not to over-furnish a small pool. Gladstoniana, the finest white variety with golden stamens, and the beautiful and fragrant Rose Nymph both need a large pool. The blood-red Froebeli, a popular variety, manages with less space, while Sunrise, the finest of the yellows, is usually a hesitant grower unlikely to trespass.

All members of the Laydekeri section, *Nymphaea pygmaea alba,* the smallest of the whites, soft yellow *N. pygmaea helvola,* the perfect miniature, and Pink Opal, that lifts its head just above water level, will settle down happily in small pools.

Marginal Plants
Pontederia, particularly desirable for its light blue flowers, thrives in 2 to 3 in. of water. The yellow flag, *Iris pseuda-corus,* and the blue *Iris laevigata* are happy aquatic subjects, enjoying up to an inch or so of water round their feet. The bright yellow marsh marigold, *Caltha palustris,* the water forget-me-not *Myosotis palustris,* and lysichitum, the exciting yellow Skunk Cabbage, will all grow in up to 2 in. of water or in boggy ground at the water's edge.

Moisture-loving Plants
Among those thriving in moist but not waterlogged conditions are the hemerocallis, the day lily, hostas, ferns, *Primula florindae,* trilliums, and trollius; *Leucojum aestivum,* the Summer Snowflake, will also enjoy and decorate the waterside. Astilbes, in new pinks and reds, will give a delightful performance just above water level. Lastly, *Lobelia cardinalis,* with its distinguished bearing, polished leaves and pillar-box scarlet flowers, revels in moisture and is too precious to be missed.

Bulbs

There are similarities between the bulb, corm and tuber: a rough guide is given here as to some of their habits and differences.

A bulb, such as a narcissus or hyacinth, is composed of a number of fleshy scales tightly packed on top of one another. These scales are the thickened bases of the leaves with an embryo flower at the centre.

A corm is a thickened stem and is solid flesh throughout, with the embryo flower bud on the surface at the corm's apex. Examples are the gladiolus and the crocus. The corm is covered by membranous sheaths, and it is these which distinguish it from a tuber, which is also solid flesh but without the sheaths. The tuber may be either a swollen stem or swollen root. The stem bears buds known as 'eyes', as in the potato, and the root throws up growths from a crown. The dahlia and the begonia belong to this group.

The important factor in common between bulbs, corms and tubers is their food storage capacity which allows them to remain dormant without injury for long periods during the winter months when growing conditions are unsuitable.

Planning
The plan can be formal or informal. Growing daffodils in grass and woodland in their natural conditions is perhaps the happiest way of planting, and is also labour saving. To my mind no bulb is better suited to naturalising than the Pheasant's Eye narcissus.

Drifts, rather than regimented lines, are always more pleasing, though I confess I still adore a formal bed of forget-me-nots interplanted with fat, pink double tulips. The old practice of throwing a handful of bulbs on the ground and planting them where they chance to fall often works out quite well.

The low-growing bulbs are excellent for the front of the shrubbery or rock garden and will transform a dull corner.

It should be remembered that once the bulbs are over they are apt to look blousy and depressing. The foliage should be left to die down naturally, as it is through the

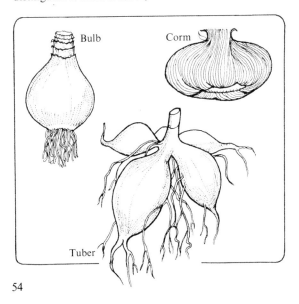

Bulb Corm

Tuber

A collection of spring-flowering bulbs, daffodils, muscari and erythroniums, form a delightful carpet in this woodland setting. Spring bulbs are especially attractive when planted in natural surroundings

leaves that the bulb builds up nourishment for the next year's flowering. Bulbs should be planted so that, when they have lost their glory, they may at least be partially hidden by the summer foliage of their neighbours.

Cultivation
There are few cultural rules in bulb growing. Good drainage is important, but on no account must the bulbs be allowed to dry out. The addition of leafmould, compost, peat or hop manure to the soil suits them well. A cushion of silver sand at the base of the bulb is helpful on heavy soils when planting lilies, gladioli and others vulnerable to dampness. Animal manure must be thoroughly rotted before use: bonemeal and hoof and horn applied at the rate of 4 oz. to the square yard will be appreciated in the autumn. The depth of planting will vary according to the type of bulb. As a rough guide, if the soil above the bulb is of the same depth as the bulb itself, measured from the base to shoulder, the gardener will not go far wrong. There are certain exceptions to this rule, such as the lilies, depending on the different species.

Bulbs are best taken out of their bags and planted on arrival: left in the bag they deteriorate quickly.

Aftercare
Once the flowers have faded the flower heads should be removed and the foliage left to die back naturally. There is always danger in digging a bed when the bulbs have died back completely, leaving nothing to mark their presence. When weeding, it is safer to use a hoe than a fork.

Lifting
Few spring bulbs require lifting other than the tulip. However, narcissi often have to be moved to make way for summer bedding plants. They should be lifted with as much soil round their roots as possible and heeled in (placed in a trench and covered with soil) out of sight in the vegetable

garden or a reserve border where the foliage can die back naturally. They should be replanted in late August in their flowering positions for the following year. Tulips should be cleaned, dried off and stored since they may be attacked by mice or rot if left in the ground. They can then be replanted in October.

Begonias, gladioli and ranunculuses are best lifted in the autumn. They should be wiped clean, laid in trays and stored for the winter in an airy, frost-proof place until planting time in spring.

Warning
When buying bulbs the beginner should order whenever possible from a bulb specialist.

Unless the bulb has been carefully and professionally handled the previous year and is healthy and solid, with the embryo bloom safely tucked in its centre, the most gifted of gardeners cannot make it bloom. Bargain offers made late in the season are as a rule an unsatisfactory buy.

The Spring Bulb Parade
The Winter Aconite (eranthis) is the first bulb of the year and heralds the snowdrop. Then come the early irises followed by the narcissi, scillas and squills, which make way for the tulips in April and May.

While trees are still in bud bulbs have no objection to growing beneath their light shade, and leucojum, fritillaria, Dog's-tooth Violet, *Anemone blanda* and miniature cyclamen will enjoy the cover.

A LIST OF SPRING BULBS FOR THE GARDEN
Chionodoxa (Glory of the Snow). Bright and dark blue, and white. There is also a pink variety. 6 in. March.
Convallaria (Lily of the Valley). Not really a spring bulb since when retarded and grown in the greenhouse it will present itself on Christmas day. 6 in. March.
Crocus. The distinguished species are even more desirable than the flamboyant Dutch forms.
Eranthis (Winter Aconite). Yellow flower with a frilly green collar. 3 to 4 in. January–March.
Erythronium (Dog's-tooth Violet). *Erythronium dens-canis.* Flowers variable from white to pink. 6 in. Spring.
Fritillaria (Snake's Head, Fritillary). Hanging bell flowers, creamy white to purple, rose and lilac: remarkably graceful. 12 to 18 in. May.
Galanthus (Snowdrop). White and green; single and double forms. 6 in. January–March.
Hyacinth. Grand satisfying trusses of Victorian opulence in all colours with heavy scent. 1 ft. Spring.
Iris. Bright golden and purple-blue dwarf. *Iris reticulata* includes a richer violet than any other spring bulb. 6 in. February.
Muscari (Grape Hyacinth). Various shades of blue and the seldom seen white variety. 6 in. April.
Narcissus. Trumpet flowers; white, yellow (including bicolors), primrose and more recently, pink. Among

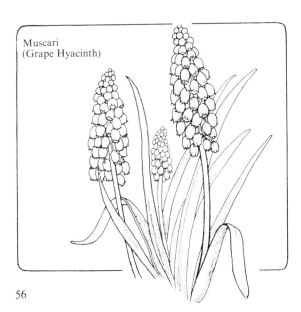

Muscari
(Grape Hyacinth)

outstanding varieties are Golden Harvest, Rembrandt, pure white Beersheba and Mount Hood. These have surpassed dear King Alfred who reigned for so long. There are also the large and small-cupped doubles; Triandrus varieties with graceful drooping flowers; Cyclamineus hybrids distinguished by their swept-back petals; Jonquils, early and delicately fragrant; the bunch-flowered Polyanthus or Tazetta group which includes the famous Soleil D'Or, and Paper White; the Poeticus, remembering the old Pheasant's Eye with white perianth (petals) and deep red eye, and the miniatures, among them the little Hooped Petticoat daffodil, a rich golden yellow with rush-like foliage, only 3 to 4 in.

Sparaxis (African Harlequin Flower). Red with yellow pencilling, black at base. 1 to 2 ft. May.

Tulip. The diversity of the tulip family and its range of colour is surprising. The species *Tulipa kaufmanniana* and such other beauties as the scarlet-vermilion, black-based bordered yellow *T. fosteriana* Red Emperor, should not be missed.

The sturdy Early Singles, the Doubles with a look of the full-blown rose and the well-known Darwins on stiff stems bearing handsome, globular flowers, are the best known of the genus and are seen in the parks in the spring in their thousands.

The Lily-flowered tulips with reflex pointed petals are perhaps the most elegant of the tribe: brownish-red Queen of Sheba with an orange marginal band, pink Mariette and white Triumphator are a great trio.

The May-flowering Cottage tulips, Rembrandts streaked and 'broken-flowered' in colour, the amusing Parrots, the Late Doubles with a look of the peony, the green-shaded Viridifloras, the pets of the flower arranger, and the multi-flowered newcomers with three or four flowers on one stem, are a few of the many.

SUMMER BULBS, TUBERS AND FLESHY-ROOTED PLANTS

Allium. The ornamental garlic. Round heads of blue, rose or carmine, solid or tasselled. 6 in. to 3 ft. May–July.

Alstroemeria (Peruvian Lily). Orange, and Ligtu hybrids in lovely shades of pink. 2 to 3 ft. June–July.

Amaryllis. *Amaryllis belladonna.* Bulbous plant not truly hardy. Should be grown against a warm south wall. Pink umbels of large, trumpet-shaped flowers. 21 in. September–October.

Anemone. St Brigid and de Caen, in rich colours. 7 to 10 in. Spring to autumn.

Begonia (Tuberous-rooted). White, pink, red, orange and yellow. 5 to 6 in. June–October.

Crocosmia. *Crocosmia masonorum.* Yellow, orange, and crimson decoratively spotted. 3 ft. *Crocosmia crocosmiiflora* the common montbretia of gardens. Earlham hybrids are colourful but require winter protection of dry litter, if not lifted. Late summer.

Cyclamen. *Cyclamen neapolitanum.* Hardy autumn flowering. White and pink with silver marbled foliage. 3 to 5 in.

Lilium regale

Eremurus (Foxtail Lily). White, pink, orange and yellow. 3 to 6 ft. May–July.

Fritillaria (Crown Imperial). *Fritillaria imperialis.* Yellow and orange. 2 to 3 ft. May.

Galtonia (Spire Lily). Often known as *Hyacinthus candicans.* White. 3 to 4 ft. Late summer.

Gladiolus. Large, miniature and butterfly flowered in a great variety of colours. 18 in. to 4 ft. July–August.

Ixia. White, red, orange or yellow. 2 ft. May–June.

Lilium. White, pink, red, yellow. 3 to 6 ft. Summer. *Lilium regale* is an ideal beginner's lily: white, the back of the petals streaked brown. July.

Montbretia See Crocosmia

Ground-cover Plants

The upkeep of a garden can be a problem these days if the gardener has neither the time nor strength to do the work himself. Without help, many a gardener is tempted to put in ground-cover plants to reduce the need for digging and weeding.

Roses, herbaceous and foliage plants, perennials—some of them rampers and smotherers, others carpet makers and ground huggers—low-growing and prostrate shrubs will serve as willing maids of all work.

The plants chosen must be vigorous enough to beat the weeds, tough enough to enjoy indifferent conditions, poor soil and partial shade, and capable of travelling fast. Perennial weeds must be pulled up before the ground cover is planted as it is difficult to get rid of them once the carpet has formed.

Here is a list of some of the weed suppressors:

Acaena. Bronze foliage, red burr-like fruits in late summer and autumn. 2 in.

Ajuga. *Ajuga reptans brockbankii.* Blue bugle flower. 6 in. June.

Alchemilla (Lady's Mantle). *Alchemilla mollis* with sulphur-green flowers. 1 to 1½ ft. July.

Bergenia (Elephant's Ears). *Bergenia cordifolia.* Pink or magenta: splendid new German hybrids. 1 ft. Spring.

Calluna (Ling or Heather). A lime-free soil and sunshine are essential to this subject. *Calluna vulgaris* varieties have rich-coloured foliage. *C.v. alba plena* has white flowers, bright green foliage. 9 to 18 in. July–October.

Campanula. *Campanula poscharskyana.* Profuse bright blue flowers. 1 ft. June.

Cornus (Creeping Dogwood). *Cornus canadensis.* White-bracted flowers: flat rosette foliage. The perfect carpeting plant. 6 in. May.

Cotoneaster. *Cotoneaster horizontalis.* A flat-growing, red-berried shrub with fan-shaped branches which defeat weeds. 3 ft.

Cytisus. *Cytisus procumbens.* Fast-growing shrub with cheerful yellow flowers. An attractive choice for a dry bank. 2 ft. May–July.

Dryas. *Dryas octopetala.* Evergreen creeping shrub with large white flowers in early summer. A lime hater. 3 in. June.

Epimedium. Yellow, crimson and white spring flowers. 6 to 12 in. April.

Erica (Heath). *Erica carnea.* Crimson, winter-flowering. If grown on lime soil frequent dressings of peat should be added. Good for a dry bank. 6 to 12 in.

Euonymus. *Euonymus fortunei variegatus.* Dense evergreen carpet. White-edged foliage pink-tinted in winter. 1 ft.

Fatshedera. *Fatshedera lizei.* Not hardy and requires a warm corner and a mild climate. Handsome shiny foliage, useful for an awkward corner or bank. 4 ft.

Geranium. *Geranium endressii.* Pink flowering; suitable for shady positions and goes well with variety Johnson's Blue. 9 to 12 in. Summer.

Hedera (Ivy). An attractive covering for bare ground where grass fails to grow.

Hedera canariensis gold and silver Silver Queen, and white-edged Glacier, interplanted with German miniature green and gold Jubilee (recently renamed Goldheart) make a decorative pattern.

Hosta (Funkia, Plantain Lily). Deciduous plant with lilac flowers and large green, glaucous, sulphur-coloured and variegated leaves. *Hosta lancifolia aurea* with golden-tinged foliage is a favourite of mine. 2 to 3 ft.

Hypericum (St John's Wort or Rose of Sharon). Bright yellow flowers, ideal for a dry bank or shady places. *Hypericum patulum* Hidcote, the outstanding member of the family, is a useful chalk lover. 2½ ft. or more. July–October.

Lamium. *Lamium galeobdolon* and *L. maculatum aureum.* Mauve or yellow flowers, attractive variegated foliage. 1 ft. Summer.

Pernettya. Evergreen shrub. White, pink or red berries. A lime hater. 2 to 5 ft.

Potentilla. Yellow flowers; the dwarf and prostrate shrubby forms bloom profusely when happy. A good choice for a dry bank. 2 to 3 ft. Summer.

Rhododendron. Bluebird and Blue Tit are charming slow-growing forms. 3 ft.

Hosta
(Plantain Lily)

The fragrant shrub rose Constance Spry contrasts well with the herbaceous geranium Johnson's Blue, an effective ground-cover plant

Strawberry. Alpine strawberry with delicious fruit. 3 in.

Tiarella (Foam Flower). *Tiarella cordifolia.* Fluffy cream flowers; thrives in shade and moist conditions. 9 in. May–September.

Viburnum. *Viburnum davidii.* Evergreen shrub of compact habit. Attractive turquoise blue berries; leathery foliage.

Vinca (Periwinkle). Carpet-forming shrub growing in sun or shade. White, blue or purple flowers; fast growing but requires control. Summer.

Perhaps I should warn the gardener that some galloping ground-cover plants, in their turn, need a firm hand, otherwise they may oust their less pushing fellows.

Trees, Shrubs, Hedges and Climbers

Planting

The planting time for trees, shrubs, hedging plants and climbers depends on whether they are deciduous, losing their leaves in the autumn and presenting fresh foliage in the spring, or evergreen, remaining in leaf throughout the year.

Deciduous trees and shrubs should be planted at any time after leaf fall, between October and March, while the plants are dormant, provided the ground is in suitable condition and not sodden or frostbound. Broad-leaved evergreens are best moved in October or in April or May just as growth is about to begin, to give the roots a good chance to become quickly established before too much moisture is lost through the leaves. This is not so important with fine-leaved conifers, which may be treated in the same way as deciduous trees and shrubs. Plants bought from garden centres in containers may be introduced at any time of the year so long as the root ball is kept intact.

Trees and shrubs should be planted as soon as they arrive from the nursery. If, however, the ground is frozen, wet or soggy, they may be stored with the roots still in their packing in a frost-proof place, or heeled in–placed in a trench with the roots lightly covered with soil–until the weather breaks.

To give the plant a good start the ground should be thoroughly prepared by double digging and working in some well-rotted manure. It will not be so easy to feed the tree or shrub once it is planted. Planting should be done on a mild day when the soil is neither too wet nor frozen.

The planting hole should be wide enough to accommodate outspread roots and the tree or shrub should be planted at the same depth as it was in its nursery bed, which can be judged from the soil mark on the stem. Broken or damaged roots should be removed before placing the plant in the planting hole, and a strong wooden stake should first be driven in 2 in. away from the main stem. The tree is then held in position and the soil replaced round the roots and well firmed in. The main stem is tied to its stake to prevent wind rocking. Plastic ties which are adjustable are recommended to allow for later growth.

Hedging shrubs may be planted either in single or double lines, the second row being staggered beside the first. The plants should be spaced 12 to 18 in. apart for most deciduous hedges, yew and holly, and 2 to 2½ ft. apart for conifers.

Climbers should be planted 1 ft. away from a wall or fence; if placed too close the roots will be deprived of moisture.

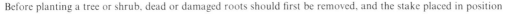

Before planting a tree or shrub, dead or damaged roots should first be removed, and the stake placed in position

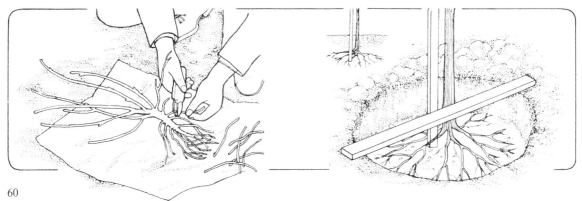

Support will be needed for the majority of climbers, either from wires attached to the wall by galvanised wall eyes or by wall nails with heads of soft leaden strips which are easily bent round the plant's stem. A climber can be assisted in growing up a tree stump, pole or pillar if the support is covered with wire netting, but should be allowed to do much as it pleases, having a natural charm when hanging down.

Aftercare

Never let the tree or shrub dry out during dry spells until it is well established and able to look after itself. Particular care should be taken to see that it does not lack water during a dry spring or early summer. Evergreens and conifers will benefit if their leaves are sprayed with water.

A 3-in. deep mulch of well-rotted manure, spent hops or peat applied during a mild period in spring should be given annually. Grass should not be allowed to grow round the stems for four or five years; the marginal ring can be assigned to spring and autumn crocuses.

Newly planted trees and shrubs must be regularly inspected during the winter. They may be lifted out of the ground by a severe frost, leaving the roots exposed. The stem should be held and the soil trodden into place.

Pruning

Care must be taken when pruning that the natural habit of the tree or shrub is not spoiled. Dead and diseased branches should be removed and cuts of over half an inch in diameter painted with a good proprietary wound dressing. Prunus species (cherries and plums) are vulnerable to silver-leaf disease and, should any pruning be necessary, it is best done during the growing period between May and July when wounds will heal over quickly.

The pruning of deciduous shrubs is related to their flowering time. Moderate pruning and thinning out, removing dead and unwanted wood, is usually all that is needed for all except the rampant. The majority, flowering before mid-summer on the previous year's growth, should be pruned as soon as the blossoms fade. Flowering shoots with faded blooms may be cut back to strong growth; weak and straggling growth should be removed. Some vigorous shrubs, such as the flamboyant forsythia, will need a firm hand to keep them under control and will benefit from cutting back to within a bud or two of the old wood.

Shrubs flowering in late summer on growth made in the current year may be cut back to within 6 in. of the old wood in January or February. Buddleia and hydrangeas respond to being cut back to within a few inches of ground level in late March.

Evergreens need little attention, unless used for hedging when they should be trimmed in spring. Unless grown as an informal hedge, berberis, flowering in April, should be trimmed after the blossom has faded, though this will mean sacrificing the berries. Strong-growing hedges, such as privet, must be regularly trimmed or they will soon lose their shape. Yew and holly hedges may be cut square at the

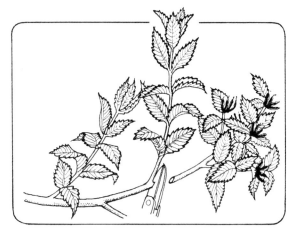
After flowering, shoots may be cut back to strong growth

top, but tall hedges of less resistant growth are better rounded or pointed at the top, especially in districts where heavy snowfalls are to be expected and the weight of snow may distort the hedge's shape.

When establishing climbers, the plant's leader should be allowed to ascend without interference until it has reached the desired height. Meanwhile, young shoots may be pinched out to within five buds of the base to encourage branching and side growths can be pruned back in August.

Pruning clematis is often confusing to the novice, the correct method and timing depending upon the variety.

Those which bloom late in the season, such as purple Jackmanii and the Viticella varieties, flower on the current year's growth. They should be pruned in February or March, either by cutting the whole plant back to within a foot or so of the ground or by pruning each young growth to within a pair of buds of its base.

Those which flower before July, such as the Montana species and many of the lovely large-flowered hybrids, bloom on the previous year's wood and may be left unpruned. The secateurs should only be used to prevent the plant getting into a hopeless tangle. The oldest vines should be thinned out and the young ones shortened after flowering.

Some shrubs, such as buddleia, respond to hard pruning

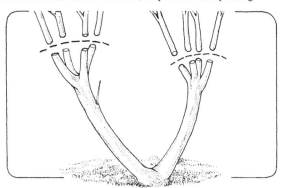

For pruning purposes secateurs are the best tool for the novice; in the hands of the inexperienced a pruning knife can do more harm than good. Shears are helpful in trimming back ivy and heather. It is important that cutting tools should be kept clean and sharp. Blunt shears and secateurs are tiring to use and bruising to plant stems, causing damage which may allow access to disease.

Over-pruning should be avoided. When in doubt put the knife away.

TREES

Planting a tree is always an exciting event. All being well it will be a permanent and dominant feature in the garden, standing resolute while generations of gardeners come and go. On this occasion we are planting not only for ourselves but our sons and successors. How tall will the tree be in fifty years? This is a planting that requires thought, imagination and careful siting.

The choice of tree will depend on taste and whether the gardener wishes for spring or summer blossom, autumn tints, or all-the-year-round colour. He will also have to decide between the deciduous and the evergreen.

There is usually a good reason for planting a tree. It is an attractive idea to plant an oak, or in the case of a small garden a pink magnolia to mark a birth or coming of age; but more often than not a tree is planted to mask an ugly building or eyesore, or to give privacy from neighbours.

The tree will give the garden a new look and contour and, in years to come, will break the skyline; the chestnut will offer shade, the acers and purple Norway maple will provide generous colour, while the flat-topped Lebanon cedar will help to furnish a barren estate. Each has its place.

The heights given in the following list can only be approximate, since much will depend on the varying conditions of climate and soil. It should be remembered, too, that many of these trees are not native to this country and may reach only half the height they would normally attain on their native soil. Most trees are slow growing, and it will be very many years before they reach maturity. The figures, therefore, represent the average height the tree might be expected to reach in British gardens ranging up to the maximum height for the species, given ideal conditions.

I hope this list of trees will help the gardener to make the right choice.

Deciduous

Acer (Maple). *Acer negundo variegatum.* Green and white. 20 to 40 ft.
   A. palmatum, the Japanese maple, striking red autumnal colouring. 10 to 20 ft.
Aesculus (Horse Chestnut). Pink, red or white flowered species. 30 to 80 ft. May.
Amelanchier, White spring flowers, purple berries, autumn tints. 20 to 30 ft.
Betula (Birch). White bark, graceful foliage. There is a weeping form. 25 to 50 ft.
Catalpa (Indian Bean). *Catalpa bignonioides.* White

flowers. *C.b. aurea* is a splendid yellow form. Ideal for the small garden. 25 to 40 ft. July.
Cercis (Judas Tree). Purple or rose flowers on bare branches. 15 to 40 ft. April.
Cornus. *Cornus kousa chinensis.* Creamy white flowers, May to June. One of the most beautiful trees. 15 to 30 ft. *C. mas*, with small yellow spring flowers in February–March, is also desirable. 12 to 16 ft.
Crataegus (Hawthorn; May). White, double scarlet or pink. 15 to 20 ft. May.
Davidia (Handkerchief Tree). Large, creamy white bracts. 20 to 65 ft. May.
Fagus (Beech). Green, copper or purple-leaved varieties. 40 to 80 ft.
Ginkgo (Maidenhair Tree). *Ginkgo biloba.* Elegant foliage, attractive autumn tints. 30 to 80 ft.
Halesia (Snowdrop Tree). White flowers followed by winged seed. 15 to 20 ft. May.
Laburnum. *Laburnum vossii* is the best of the laburnums with the longest of yellow racemes. Spring. 16 to 20 ft.
Liquidambar (Sweet Gum). Magnificent autumn colour. 30 to 80 ft.
Malus (Crab). Pink and white spring flowers; Japanese, crimson red crab and other varieties. 16 to 25 ft.
Populus (Poplar). Erect green column with widely spreading roots which can become dangerous to buildings. 40 to 70 ft.
Prunus. Gigantic genus which includes the ornamental and Japanese cherry, peach, plum, almond, 15 to 30 ft.; and the delightful *Prunus subhirtella autumnalis*, the autumn and winter cherry, pink, flowering intermittently from November to March. 16 to 30 ft.
Pyrus. *Pyrus salicifolia,* the Willow-leaved Pear. White flowers. 16 to 30 ft. Spring.
Quercus (Oak and Scarlet Oak). Wonderful autumn colour. 40 to 80 ft.
Robinia (False Acacia). *Robinia pseudoacacia* Frisia, the striking golden variety with ferny foliage, is a superb tree. 7 to 20 ft.
Salix (Willow). *Salix vitellina pendula,* a fine golden-leaved weeping form that thrives on moist land. 40 to 50 ft.
Tilia (Lime). Suitable for pleaching. Dislikes an exposed situation. 60 to 80 ft.

Evergreen

Arbutus (Strawberry Tree). Small white flowers and red fruit, autumn. 20 ft.
Cedrus (Cedar). *Cedrus atlantica glauca,* the Blue Cedar, and *C.a. aurea,* the golden form. 60 to 100 ft. Also *C. deodara,* the Deodar Cedar, and *C. libani* the Cedar of Lebanon, 50 to 80 ft.

A mixed selection of shrubs, including both flowering and foliage plants, gives a well-furnished appearance to a corner of the garden and provides a feature of interest for most of the year

Chamaecyparis. *Chamaecyparis lawsoniana*, Lawson's Cypress, forming blue, green or grey columns. There are many dwarf and slow-growing varieties, some suitable for the rock garden. 6 to 100 ft.

Cupressocyparis. *Cupressocyparis leylandii* is the fastest growing cypress we possess, forming an excellent screen. 40 to 50 ft.

Eucalyptus (Gum Tree). Blue-grey foliage; a fast grower. Most species dislike lime and will not withstand cold winds. 20 to 60 ft.

Libocedrus. *Libocedrus decurrens*, the Incense Cedar. Columnar form. 50 to 70 ft.

Magnolia. *Magnolia grandiflora*. The only evergreen magnolia. White, heavily scented flowers. Requires protection. 15 to 20 ft.

Picea (Spruce). *Picea abies*, the Christmas tree. 40 to 100 ft. *P. pungens glauca*, the Blue Spruce, blue-grey. 30 ft.

Taxus. *Taxus baccata fastigiata*, the Irish Yew. Dark green column; also a golden form.

SHRUBS

Shrubs are a framework to a garden whether they are deciduous or evergreen. Deciduous flowering shrubs keep the garden gay in spring, while evergreens furnish shrubbery and beds throughout the winter.

There is a tendency to plant shrubs too close together, and a gardener often lives to blame himself for this mistake. He would do far better to come to terms with bare ground for a few years rather than be forced to prune cruelly to avoid overcrowding.

The majority of shrubs are unfussy, but rhododendrons, azaleas, camellias and certain ericas are lime haters. Soil can be made more palatable to this group by applications of sequestrene or acid peat but the lime haters will never really appreciate an alkaline soil.

Deciduous

Azalea. Exbury and Knaphill hybrids. Palest yellow, orange and crimson. 2½ ft. May–June.

Berberis. *Berberis thunbergii*. Yellow flowers followed by red fruits, purple foliage. 4 to 6 ft. April–May.

Buddleia. White, mauve, purple. July. *Buddleia globosa*, orange. 10 to 12 ft. May–June.

Caryopteris. Blue flowers, grey-green foliage. 4 ft. August–October.

Cotoneaster. *Cotoneaster horizontalis*. White flowers, fine red berries. Popular fish-bone prostrate shrub. 3 ft. May.

Cytisus. White and yellow sun lovers. Sometimes short lived. *Cytisus battandieri*, yellow, pineapple-scented flowers; a grand plant when grown against a wall. 5 to 12 ft. June.

Daphne. Purple; lovely scent. 3 ft. Spring.

Deutzia. White and purple. Good town plant. 4 to 8 ft. June.

Euonymus. *Euonymus europaeus*. Brilliant autumn hues. White and scarlet fruits. 6 to 15 ft.

Forsythia. A choice of yellow and golden varieties. 6 to 10 ft. March–April.

Fuchsia. Hardy varieties such as *Fuchsia magellanica riccartonii*. Red. 3 to 10 ft. Summer.

Genista. Yellow. 8 to 10 ft. July. *Genista lydia* is particularly beautiful. 2 ft. May–June.

Hamamelis (Witch Hazel). *Hamamelis mollis*. Yellow. 8 to 12 ft. January–February.

Hibiscus. *Hibiscus syriacus*. White, blue, pink and red. 3 to 6 ft. August–September.

Hydrangea. White, blue, pink and red. *Hydrangea macrophylla*. Hortensia and lace-cap varieties. 3 to 5 ft. July.

Hypericum. *Hypericum patulum*. Yellow. 3 to 5 ft. July–August.

Kolkwitzia. Pink. Foxglove-shaped flowers with yellow throats. 5 ft. June.

Lilac See Syringa

Magnolia. White and pink. *Magnolia stellata* and *M. soulangiana* both easy and free flowering. 6 to 15 ft. Spring.

Paeonia (Tree Peony). Pink, red and purple. 4 to 6 ft. May–June.

Philadelphus (Mock Orange). White, white and purple. 3 to 15 ft. June.

Potentilla. *Potentilla fruticosa*. Shrubby cinquefoil. Yellow. 2 to 4 ft. Summer.

Rhus. *Rhus typhina*, Stag's Horn Sumach. Highly coloured autumn foliage. 15 to 20 ft.

Ribes. Flowering currant. White, pink and crimson. 6 ft. Early spring.

Rosa See p. 33

Spiraea. White, pink and crimson. 3 to 8 ft. Spring and summer varieties.

Syringa (Lilac). White, mauve and purple. Heavily scented. 6 to 20 ft. May–June.

Tamarix (Tamarisk). Pink. Thrives in coastal districts. 12 ft. July–August.

Ulex (Gorse). Golden. *Ulex europaeus plenus* is a double variety. Suitable for dry banks. 5 ft. April–May.

Viburnum. White and pink. Attractive deciduous varieties. 6 to 15 ft. May–June.

Weigela. Pink and red. *Weigela florida variegata* has cream-margined leaves. 6 to 8 ft. May–June.

Evergreen

Camellia. White, pink and red. Fine glossy foliage. 6 to 20 ft. Spring.

Ceanothus. Blue. Some of our best shrubs. Slightly tender. 3 ft. July–October.

Choisya. White, 4 to 6 ft. May–June.

Elaeagnus. *Elaeagnus pungens maculata*. Yellow and green foliage. Slow growing. 6 ft.

Erica. *Erica carnea* group. Some tolerant of lime. 1 ft. November–April.

Escallonia. White, pink and red. Thrives at seaside. 6 to 15 ft. June–September.

Garrya. *Garrya elliptica*. Glossy foliage and 6-in. catkins. 6 to 12 ft. January.

Hebe (Veronica). Free flowering, white, pink, blue, purple. 2 to 12 ft. Summer.

Kalmia. *Kalmia latifolia*, the Calico Bush. Prefers a lime-free soil. Pink. 6 to 10 ft. June.

Lavandula (Lavender). 1½ to 3 ft. July–August.

Mahonia. *Mahonia japonica*. Pendulous yellow, lily-of-the-valley-scented racemes; dark green foliage. 6 ft. February–March.

Olearia (Daisy Bush). *Olearia haastii*. Cream or white. 4 to 8 ft. July.

Pernettya. White, pink, red and purple berries. Lime hater. 2 to 5 ft.

Pieris. *Pieris formosa forrestii*. Splendid shrub. White lily-of-the-valley flowers; pink-red young growth in spring. Lime-free soil. 6 to 8 ft. March–May.

Pyracantha (Firethorn). White flowers followed by orange berries. 12 ft. June.

Rhododendron. All colours. Lime-free soil. 1 to 20 ft. March–June.

Rosmarinus (Rosemary). Blue. 1 to 5 ft. April–May.

Santolina (Lavender Cotton). Yellow. Silver-grey foliage. 1½ to 2½ ft. July–August.

Senecio. White or yellow daisy-like flowers. Silver foliage. 3 ft. July.

Skimmia. *Skimmia japonica*. White. Red berries when male and female plants present. Tolerant of semi-shade. 3 ft. Spring.

Siphonosmanthus. Usually listed as *Osmanthus delavayi*. White. 6 to 10 ft. Spring.

Viburnum. *Viburnum tinus*. White, tinged pink. 8 to 10 ft. November–April.

Yucca. Creamy white spikes. 3 to 6 ft. July–August.

HEDGES

The purpose of the hedge is the first consideration. Is it required as a windbreak, screen, barrier or boundary? Is it to be ornamental and aesthetically beautiful, or an obstacle thick enough to keep out cats, dogs and other marauders?

Much will depend on whether you require a formal or an informal hedge and there is also the question of price. Laurel and privet are reasonably cheap and privet is easy to increase. Yew and holly are more costly and slow growing. Beech and hornbeam make useful windbreaks; beech will be found to be the better of the two on wet and heavy soil. A thick hawthorn hedge will defy small boys and animals. There are shrubs which thrive at the seaside and some which are especially tough for exposed windy sites and valleys prone to frost.

A mixed hedge can be most attractive. The famous tapestry hedge at Hidcote, Gloucestershire, immediately comes to mind, made up of green and variegated holly, box, and green and copper beech.

If shoots are cut back methodically when young the hedge will be encouraged to bush out at the base. The familiar and bare-based privet hedge is usually the result of poor feeding, unsatisfactory pruning and the presence of debris and weeds that have been allowed to collect at the plant's base.

I now give a list of plants which are especially suitable for hedging. They are deciduous unless otherwise stated.

Beech See Fagus

Berberis. *Berberis stenophylla*. Evergreen with yellow flowers. Heavy pruning will reduce flowering. April–May.

Buxus (Box). Small-leaved evergreen suitable for formal hedge. Slow growing.

Carpinus (Hornbeam). Makes a good dense screen. Should be summer pruned in the third year.

Chamaecyparis. *Chamaecyparis lawsoniana*, Lawson's Cypress. Hardy evergreen conifer. Rich green. Suitable for a 6-ft. hedge.

Cotoneaster. *Cotoneaster simonsii*. Semi-evergreen berrying form; fast growing.

Crataegus (Hawthorn, May). White or pink flowers with red fruits. A useful boundary hedge. May–June.

Cupressocyparis. *Cupressocyparis leylandii*. Evergreen. The fastest growing conifer we possess, making 4 ft. of growth a year. Forms an effective windbreak.

Escallonia. Mostly evergreen. Dark foliage and pink or red flowers. Happy in coastal districts. Summer.

Fagus (Beech). Recommended for chalky soil. Keeps well furnished at base if clipped at the end of February.

Hornbeam See Carpinus

Ilex (Holly). Dark green and variegated silver and golden forms. Evergreen. Slow growing until established. Female plants bear the berries.

Lavandula (Lavender). Grey-foliaged dwarf hedge. Should be pruned in early spring to avoid interference with flowering. July.

Laurel See Prunus

Ligustrum (Privet). Evergreen. Green or gold foliage. The green is particularly quick growing. Seldom given the attention it deserves, gardeners trading on its good nature.

Lilac See Syringa

Lonicera (Honeysuckle). *Lonicera nitida*. Evergreen shrubby honeysuckle. Makes a compact low hedge of dense form.

Mahonia. *Mahonia aquifolium*. Glossy green leaves; yellow flowers in early spring. Makes an attractive, medium-sized evergreen hedge.

Privet See Ligustrum

Prunus. *Prunus laurocerasus* (Laurel). Solid and quick-growing evergreen. Content in almost any situation.

Rhododendron. For lime-free soils only. *Rhododendron ponticum*. Large shrub with mauve to lilac-pink flowers. May–June. *R. luteum* makes a lovely yellow-flowering hedge. May.

Syringa (Lilac). White, mauve and purple. Informal light hedge often seen in Denmark. May–June.

Thuja. *Thuja plicata*. A good 8- to 9-ft. evergreen hedge that will tolerate clipping.

Ulex (Gorse). Golden. *Ulex europaeus plenus* is a double variety. Windbreak which will defeat trespassers. April–May.

Yew. Evergreen. The most distinguished of hedges: slow growing, lasting, and a becoming background to flower borders. Highly poisonous to horses and cattle.

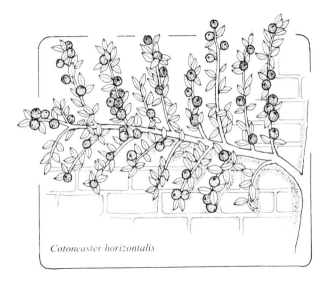

Cotoneaster horizontalis

CLIMBERS

Few climbers are equipped to cling and climb without support, other than the ivy, Virginia Creeper, *Hydrangea petiolaris* and *Schizophragma integrifolium*. But there are quite a number of plants with tendrils, spines and aerial roots which, given a helping hand, will twine themselves in and out of a supporting trellis. There are also some shrubs which, though not strictly climbers, are particularly suitable for growing against a wall.

There are climbers for all aspects: the sunny south and south-west walls should be reserved for your favourites. Camellias often do well on an east wall and the Morello Cherry, pyracantha, *Hydrangea petiolaris* (a self-clinger) usually succeed when facing north.

Most climbers have a healthy appetite and the soil should be well dug and enriched if they are to travel far. A taste of dried blood from time to time will increase their pace.

The following climbers are deciduous unless otherwise stated.

Actinidia. *Actinidia kolomikta.* White and pink variegated leaves. White flowers, yellow fruits. Twining. Seen at its most colourful when trained against a sunny wall. June.

Ampelopsis. *Ampelopsis brevipedunculata.* A vigorous climber with foliage similar to the hop. Porcelain-blue small grapes after a hot summer.

Ceanothus. Can be trained against a wall. Slightly tender. Evergreen and deciduous varieties.

Clematis. Species, and large-flowered hybrids. Twining. Spring and summer flowering.

Chaenomeles (Ornamental Quince). Syn. *Cydonia japonica.* Can be trained against a wall. Pink, red and scarlet. Spring.

Cotoneaster. *Cotoneaster horizontalis.* White flowers followed by red berries. June.

Hedera (Ivy). Insignificant green flowers. Self-clinging evergreen with attractive variegated forms.

Hydrangea. *Hydrangea petiolaris.* White. Self-clinging climber. Does best on a north wall. June.

Jasminum. *Jasminum nudiflorum,* the Winter Jasmine. Yellow. Excellent 'climber' for a north or east wall. November–February. *Jasminum officinale.* White, very fragrant. Vigorous climber. Summer.

Kerria. *Kerria japonica.* Yellow. Graceful wall plant. April–May.

Lonicera (Honeysuckle). Twining. Yellow, orange, red. Not all varieties are fragrant. Effective rambling over other shrubs. June–July.

Magnolia. *Magnolia grandiflora.* Evergreen shrub with white, fragrant flowers. A fine wall plant needing plenty of space. Summer.

Polygonum. *Polygonum baldschuanicum,* the Russian Vine, or Mile-a-minute Climber. White. Invasive climber which must be controlled. July–October.

Pyracantha (Firethorn). Evergreen wall shrub. White flowers followed by orange berries. June.

Rosa (Rose). Climbers and ramblers. Mme Gregoire Staechelin, with carmine buds opening white, is very lovely. Perpetual flowering group bloom generously throughout the summer.

Solanum. *Solanum crispum,* the Chilean potato. Purple and yellow. Free flowering in mild districts. July–September. Can be trained against a wall.

Vitis (Vine). Tendril climbers with red and crimson autumn tints. Require space. *Vitis coignetiae* is a particularly grand Japanese species, presenting glorious autumn colour.

Wisteria. Twining. Mauve, white and purple drooping racemes, very fragrant. Unfortunately in some districts it is necessary to protect the flower buds against birds.

Patio and Porch

WINDOW BOXES

The window box is the most intimate and companionable of gardens, and as enthralling as a slow-motion picture. The gardener can watch a flower unfold as he drinks his morning coffee and close as he smokes a final cigarette.

There is a wide range of boxes of which the traditional Italian pink moulded terracotta is the most distinguished. A box can also be made of galvanised iron, of plastic composition or of wood, but ideally it should have adequate drainage holes and be of a suitable size to fit the space available. If the box is wooden, it should be of well-seasoned hardwood which will not warp, and treated inside with a wood preservative–but not creosote, which is harmful to plants.

A well-made box when filled with soil can be very heavy, and it is important to see that it is firmly bolted or secured in position by brackets before being filled. It is advisable to raise the box on small blocks to allow free drainage.

Filling the Box

The drainage holes should be covered with crocks to prevent them becoming clogged by soil, and a further layer of drainage material such as pebbles, broken bricks or weathered clinker added. A substantial layer of damp peat and roughage over the crocks is a life saver, as it helps to retain moisture and prevents soil from seeping through and blocking the drainage holes.

A good compost is vital, since plants grown in containers need a richer diet than can be provided by ordinary garden soil. John Innes Compost No. 2 or 3 or one of the peat-based composts are suitable. The gardener is advised to change the soil in his box at least every other year. Roots cannot cling to played-out soil in which no nourishment or substance is left. If the soil is retained, a dressing of John Innes Base Fertiliser at the rate of 4 oz. per bushel of soil should be added to give it new life before fresh plants are put in.

Firm the soil lightly with the fingers, distributing it evenly in the corners, and leaving a good inch below the level of the box to allow room for watering.

Planting

Firm planting is essential, provided the soil is not compacted. A narrow-bladed trowel or two-pronged fork are the most useful planting tools. The heights and spread of the plants should be considered before planting so that the smaller growing ones are not smothered. Stakes and ties should be put in at this stage, and the newly planted box then watered through a fine rose.

Aftercare

It is important to keep the window box well watered in dry weather: one of the snags of growing plants in containers is the rapidity with which they dry out. Feeding with a weak liquid or seaweed-based fertiliser in the summer months will keep your plants happy, though some, such as marigolds, are inclined to be over-generous with leaves at the expense of flowers if given too rich a diet.

WHAT TO GROW

The Spring Box

It is impossible to go wrong with bulbs. Crocuses, daffodils, grape hyacinths (blue and white), hyacinths and scillas, and short-stemmed tulips, are beautiful standbys for the spring. They should be planted in September and October, and after flowering are best given to country friends and fresh bulbs bought for the box.

There are two spring bedders that never fail to mix happily with bulbs: forget-me-nots, blue, pink or white, and the primula family, polyanthus or primroses, yellow, blue, or mixed.

The Summer Box

Here the choice is tremendous. Seed is cheap but few summer annuals can be relied upon for bloom and colour on the window sill. Among the hopeful are the nasturtiums, (and I have a liking for the variety Cherry Rose), candytuft in purple, mauve and white, energetic little Canary Creeper, gentian blue *Phacelia campanularia*, godetia, Bijou and Little Sweetheart sweet peas, calendula (the daisy marigold), and mignonette.

Gardeners looking for permanent residents should turn to the perennials, aubrieta, auricula, house leeks, dwarf campanulas, the different coloured thymes, pink and white arabis, the pinks, and the saxifragas, not forgetting London Pride.

Bedding plants bought as seedlings from the market are a great help in brightening up the box. The snapdragons, fibrous-rooted begonias, Bellis daisies, dwarf French marigolds, impatiens, (Busy Lizzie), lobelia, pansies, petunias and violas are a gay band and many will flower on until the frost.

Pot plants, an ivy-leaved or zonal geranium, a sweet-scented Cherry Pie (heliotrope), fuchsia or a miniature rose can be tipped out of its pot to take the place of a former occupant.

The Autumn Box

This box is something of an extra. The China aster–chrysanthemum or peony-flowered, giant rayed, ostrich plumed, pompon or powder puff–can play a leading role. Or the dwarf chrysanthemums, among them pretty pink and white Hebe, Crimson Vulcan and popular yellow Denise, and the single-flowered Coltness dahlias will give a bright show with very little trouble.

The Winter Box

This is for those with money to spend who do not intend to plant spring bulbs, for the temporary winter box of

Spring bulbs and bedding plants blend well in a window box

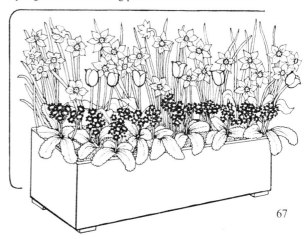

67

small and miniature shrubs is quite expensive. There is *Pernettya mucronata* Bell's Seedling, with large pink and red berries, *Ruta graveolens,* a form of the culinary rue with blue-green foliage, the compact hebes, *Elaeagnus pungens,* and *E. p. variegata* or *maculata,* splashed with gold; the variegated ivies, Glacier, Sheen Silver and Chicago, can be relied on to fill in any spare corners. If not too closely packed the shrubs can be interplanted with bulbs, and I tried out a successful mixture last year of golden heather – Golden Feather and Golden Haze – with blue grape hyacinths and scillas among them.

Plants for Special Places

The majority of plants enjoy basking in the sun, the gazania, geranium and mesembryanthemum even more than their fellows.

The tuberous begonia is happier out of full sun and is my first choice for a partially shaded position. The antirrhinum, campanulas and Creeping Jenny give quite a good account of themselves in partial shade. Although plants will grow in full shade, few will flower. Coleus, ferns, hostas, helxine, lily of the valley, London Pride, night-scented stock and dear old Busy Lizzie (impatiens) will do their best.

Hardy ferns, interplanted with Busy Lizzie, will make an attractive box. I have seen these give a good account of themselves in a London basement.

Colour Combination

For grey and silver foliage *Artemisia splendens* and *Helichrysum plicatum,* a feathery froth of silver, are almost hardy, but I can recommend *Stachys lanata,* Lamb's Ear, with grey-white nap foliage as being entirely reliable. Meanwhile Doris, with a winning shrimp eye, is the pick of the pinks.

The smooth and the rough-leaved, the dense and transparent, the highly coloured or silvery-white foliage plants, together with the variegated and scented-leaved geranium Crystal Palace Gem and golden and red tricolor Mrs Harvey Cox make a cool summer mixture.

For a real splash of colour a get-together of petunias, many coloured geraniums or lemon, yellow, orange and red antirrhinums and marigolds, will make anybody blink. Pink arabis, pink and white fibrous-rooted begonias, Cambridge blue lobelia and pink and white Bellis daises are for those looking for a restful planting.

The Herb Box

Now that British cooking is receiving more attention herbs are in the news. A six-herb box of mint, sage, rosemary, parsley, lemon thyme and French marjoram makes a good beginning.

Mint, given a rich, moist soil, survives even in built-up areas; parsley – a must in the kitchen – does best if planted in the spring.

The Salad Box

Window-box tomatoes and lettuces are usually more entertaining than commercial. Lettuce Tom Thumb and crisp, well-formed Arctic King is a good colour and decorative, and spring onions, mustard and cress and radishes should be included for good measure.

Thanks to the gardener and his window box for enlivening many a dull street.

HANGING BASKETS

Baskets have made a splendid comeback and even local authorities have taken to them. There are several types, wooden, wire or the plastic variety, in all patterns and sizes.

Perhaps I should remind beginners that when filled with soil these containers can be heavy to handle and unless there is a man at hand, a moderate-sized basket should be chosen.

Planting and Aftercare

The containers should first be packed tightly with a layer of moist sphagnum moss. If the basket is then lined with polythene pierced with drainage holes, followed by more tightly packed moist sphagnum and a layer of loam fibre, the chore of watering will be reduced.

The plants must be put in firmly using John Innes No. 1 or a peat-based compost. At least an inch should be left between the soil surface and the rim of the basket for

A flower pot provides a firm base when planting up a hanging basket. The polythene lining needs holes for drainage

watering, for exposed to the sun and the wind these containers dry out rapidly. After planting, the basket should be immersed in water and allowed to soak and then lifted out and drained off before hanging.

When the temperature is high it is a good plan to take the container down at least once a week and to soak it for a quarter of an hour in the sink. The plants will enjoy a syringe of water every evening in the hot weather, even if the soil is moist.

Arrangement

The gardener can either build up high in the centre with tall plants–fuchsias, coleus, heliotrope, marguerites, verbena or Busy Lizzie–and surround them with trailers, or fill the basket with a uniform planting such as pelargoniums or petunias, or a mixture of both.

Trailers and edgings include *Lobelia* Blue Cascade or Sapphire with its winking white eye, *Campanula isophylla*, blue or white, or, one of the best and foolproof plants for hanging baskets, the nasturtium. The nasturtium has an unfortunate reputation for being attacked by blackfly but this can be avoided by giving the plants regular preventative sprays *before* the enemy establishes itself.

Tradescantia, the Wandering Jew, the little helxine Mind-your-own-business, and nepeta (catmint) will fill up odd 'corners' at the rim.

Meanwhile, a white marguerite will always give the basket a light and airy look and a fine summer atmosphere.

TUBS

Space for a tub can often be found in a court or backyard, verandah, or on a doorstep. It has the advantage of being mobile and can be stationed in a dull part of the garden to give a splash of colour where nothing else will grow.

Tubs are available in teak, oak, earthenware, plastic, or fine-grade concrete, or a home-made tub may be constructed from a packing case, wash tub or beer barrel. Large decorative Italian terracotta containers, in good design, look well in the garden, but it must be remembered that moisture evaporates fast when these are standing in the sun.

Planting and Aftercare

The tub should be provided with drainage holes, covered with a good foundation of broken crocks or rubble. A layer of grass turves placed upside down over the crocks will prevent soil washing down and clogging the drainage holes, or a layer of damp sphagnum moss or coarse peat as roughage will serve the same purpose. John Innes No. 2 or 3 or one of the peat-based composts will satisfy the majority of shrubs but lime haters such as rhododendrons must be planted in a lime-free, peat-based compost. But however good the soil mixture, it must be regularly replenished once or twice a year by scraping away the tired surface soil and replacing it with a good loam and leaf-mould compost, to which a dressing of organic fertilisers should be added. An occasional summer feed of liquid manure will also improve the performance of the plants.

It is asking a great deal of a shrub to live permanently in the confines of a tub, and if after it has been in situ three years it shows signs of starvation, it should be lifted and replanted in fresh soil.

WHAT TO GROW

Annuals
Choose them to match the plants in the window boxes, or at least to blend with them.

Bulbs
Lilies, especially *Lilium regale* or *L. auratum*, are magnificent in tubs.

Perennials
Hardy fuchsias, the dignified acanthus, the almost tropical agapanthus, the tree peony from Japan or the prickly yucca from southern America are attractive plants for a tub.

Shrubs
Rose. Roses do not enjoy confinement but the floribundas make the best of it.

Laurus (Bay). A lustrous evergreen, happy in town and semi-shade.

Rosmarinus (Rosemary). Gives a scented welcome on the doorstep on a summer's day.

Buxus (Box) and **Taxus** (Yew). These offer the gardener a chance to practise the gentle art of topiary. A bird, a jug or teddy bear?

Camellia. An admirable shrub for a tub in towns and light shade.

Hydrangea. A great standby. Young plants flower better than old.

Chaenomeles. The reliable Japanese quince, an attractive shrub with its waxy red, flame, pink or white flowers.

Juniperus (Juniper). Silver or blue-grey, feather or columnar forms.

Rhododendron. An outstanding tub plant that gives the rhododendron and azalea fan, on alkaline soil, an opportunity to grow this lime hater.

THE PORCH

There are porches and porches. If your porch is sunless and the door is being constantly opened, it will be cold and draughty and you will have to fall back on the hardy house plants such as chlorophytum, tradescantia, the climbing *Philodendron scandens*, spring bulbs and a few hardy garden plants such as dicentra, the bedding geraniums and miniature roses.

I remember a delightful sunny porch at Swanage that was kept at a steady warmth throughout the winter and shaded with a pale green venetian blind in the summer. This porch was always full of colour and bright with bulbs, cinerarias, begonias, regal pelargoniums, petunias, schizanthus and primulas, while a backcloth of climbing *Plumbago capensis*, a sheet of sky blue, mingled with the green and purple Cup-and-saucer Plant, *Cobaea scandens*.

Heat, ventilation and shading are necessary for such a successful performance. I am glad to say that it would seem that glass porches are once more on their way in.

Vegetables

Vegetables need, but do not always get, as much attention as flowers. The site should face the sun, be as near the water supply as possible, away from large trees, and be well dug, well fed and kept free of weeds. At least a third of the plot should be dug over every year and manure or compost added.

Layout and Rotation of Crops

Any vegetable garden worthy of the name should be planned on a rotation system, the crops being moved every year so that they are never stationed in the same place two years running.

The main reason for this is that the constant planting of the same crop year after year robs the soil of certain properties and pests and diseases have the opportunity of settling in permanently. Continual planting of brassicas leads to the build up of club root disease.

The fact that some crops thrive on freshly manured land, while others respond better to land that has been manured for a previous crop when the humus has matured, makes the rotation system essential.

The simplest method of rotating crops is to divide the garden plot into three sections.

The Royal Horticultural Society has given me their kind permission to reprint the diagram that appears in their admirable publication *The Vegetable Garden Displayed*.

FIRST YEAR	SECOND YEAR	THIRD YEAR
1	1	1
Manured with dung or compost. Peas, beans, onions, leeks, tomatoes, spinach, spinach beet and celery. Succession crops–carrots, beet.	*Fertilisers.* Potatoes, carrots, beet, parsnips, swedes. Succession crops–onions, spinach, lettuces and cabbages.	*Fertilisers and lime.* Cabbages, sprouts, cauliflowers, kales, broccoli. Seed bed for green crops.
2	2	2
Fertilisers. Potatoes, carrots, beet, parsnips, swedes. Succession crops–onions, spinach, lettuces and cabbages.	*Fertilisers and lime.* Cabbages, sprouts, cauliflowers, kales, broccoli. Seed bed for green crops.	*Manured with dung or compost* Peas, beans, onions, leeks, tomatoes, spinach, spinach beet and celery. Succession crops–carrots, beet.
3	3	3
Fertilisers and lime. Cabbages, sprouts, cauliflowers, kales, broccoli. Seed bed for green crops.	*Manured with dung or compost.* Peas, beans, onions, leeks, tomatoes, spinach, spinach beet and celery. Succession crops–carrots, beet.	*Fertilisers.* Potatoes, carrots, beet, parsnips, swedes. Succession crops–onions, spinach, lettuces and cabbages.

First year: PLOT 1. For those vegetables which appreciate fresh manure and rich land.
PLOT 2. Root crops which prefer land that has been manured a year previously, plus a light dressing of artificial fertiliser.
PLOT 3. Green crops and a seed bed for green crops. This plot will benefit from a dressing of lime followed later with a light dressing of artificial fertiliser.
Second year: The three groups move on one plot: Plot 1 to Plot 3; Plot 2 to Plot 1; Plot 3 to Plot 2.
Third year: Plot 1 to Plot 2; roots to Plot 3; cabbages to Plot 1.

The cycle is now complete and the gardener, back at starting point, repeats the rotation, so that on each portion of ground he grows the same crops only once every three years.

This layout is designed with the South in mind and the northern gardener will have to modify his choice of vegetables, replacing the tomatoes, broccoli and possibly the runner beans with crops such as summer cabbages and cauliflowers. Further changes will have to be made to please family tastes. Some crops will be late in maturing, making it impossible to clear them in time for the next planting. Nature doesn't go by the book for expert or beginner.

Successional and Catch Crops

Lettuces, radishes and some others should be sown repeatedly in short rows throughout the sowing season to supply a continuous crop, avoiding a glut. Such quick-maturing crops can also be grown in ground that is later to be used for plantings of celery or winter brassicas.

Intercropping

Intercrops of lettuces can be sown between the peas; carrots and beets between various crops; they can be pulled when young leaving the regular crop to grow on and mature for storing.

Cultivation

The ground should be rich with organic matter capable of retaining moisture, but efficient drainage is important. If the soil is light and the drainage fast the humus-forming material should not be introduced until a month or so before sowing seed or it may be leached away—washed away by the rain. Clay soil should be dug in the autumn so that wind, rain and snow can play their part in breaking down the clods. Summer and autumn vegetables are the best choice for heavy clay.

Fertilisers, too, are helpful, and basic slag is first rate if applied during autumn or winter, in late January or early February, six weeks after manuring. Bonemeal, the veteran's slow-acting standby, also works well if applied early in the year.

Most vegetable gardens benefit from a dressing of lime about once in three years. With a rotational cropping system, one third of the area can be limed each year, as indicated on the chart. Lime reacts when brought into contact with some fertilisers so that valuable nitrogen is lost: several weeks should be allowed to elapse after the lime application before dressing with fertiliser in order to avoid this reaction.

Vegetables seem to enjoy a change of diet and dried blood, sulphate of ammonia or any reputable fertiliser are helpful pick-me-ups during the growing season. They should be sprinkled on the surface of the soil, avoiding foliage, and watered in.

It is best to grow those vegetables which are hard to obtain or expensive to buy, and to aim at flavour rather than size. In general, green vegetables are shallow rooting, so keep rich humus-forming material near the surface. Carrots, parsnips and turnips in particular respond to a fine tilth.

Sowing Seed

Draw the seed drills in straight lines using a garden line as a guide; should the soil be at all dry, water before sowing. A sprinkling of naphthalene along the drills will help to keep the egg-laying flies away.

The best seed available should be sown, and sowing in the South begun early in March for the first crop, at the end of the month in the Midlands and at the beginning of April in the North and in cold parts of the country. The seed should be covered lightly with fine soil. Brassicas are best raised on a seed bed and later transplanted to their permanent quarters.

Keep the garden clean, removing all debris and discoloured leaves which might harbour pests or disease and remember, generous feeding pays. You get out of the vegetable plot what you put into it.

Storing

Potatoes, beets, dahlias and other tender roots can be stored outside in a ridge-like heap, known as a clamp, or in boxes in a dark, frost-proof shed or cellar.

To construct a clamp a well-drained piece of ground must be found. A thick layer of straw or small branches and twigs should be laid down as a base, the roots placed on this and then covered with a layer of clean straw spread over with earth about 1 ft. thick and beaten smooth with the back of a spade into a steep-sided mound. Ventilation is provided by allowing wisps of straw to pass through the soil so that the warm air inside the clamp can escape.

Only healthy and undamaged roots should be stored and the gardener must take particular care to seal the clamp again when opening it for the regular examination or removal of roots for the kitchen. He must when necessary provide protection from vermin.

Cabbages can be stored for a month or so if kept in a cool, dark place.

Pests and Diseases

Greens, and in particular the brassicas (cauliflower, cabbage, Brussels sprouts) and other members of the family, are particularly vulnerable to pests and disease. But at least we know the enemy to expect on the different crops, and the insecticide and fungicide specialists will be happy to advise the beginner how to control them and keep the vegetable garden healthy.

Spraying with derris or lindane (gamma-BHC) will control aphids and caterpillars. To prevent attacks by cabbage root fly the seed bed should be dusted with lindane or the newly planted seedlings with 4 per cent. calomel dust. Affected plants should be sprayed with lindane, provided they are not to be harvested for two weeks after spraying, but it should not be used on onions, carrots or potatoes as it may taint the flavour.

Club root is a fungal disease affecting brassicas, and thrives in acid conditions. Infected plants must be burned, but the best antidote is to keep the ground well limed. Dip the roots before planting in a paste made from 4 per cent. calomel dust and water, or sprinkle calomel dust into the planting holes.

Blight, affecting potatoes and tomatoes, should be anticipated by a preventive spray of Bordeaux mixture or zineb, which should be repeated at fortnightly intervals from June to September.

If the rotation of crops is carefully followed, grubs and fungus, unable to build up their forces will, it is hoped, be starved out.

A LIST OF VEGETABLES

Beans, Broad
SEED: Sow early types 3 in. deep in November in mild districts, February to April in cold districts.
SPACING: 9 in. between plants, 24 in. between rows.
CULTIVATION: Pinch out tops when a reasonable number of pods have set to prevent blackfly.
CROPPING: June–August.

Beans, French
SEED: Sow 2 in. deep in April under glass for transplanting after risk of frost is past, or May–July in the open.
SPACING: 9 to 12 in. between plants, 18 in. between single rows, 24 in. between double rows.
CULTIVATION: Pick young to keep the plants cropping.
CROPPING: July–October.

Beans, Runner
SEED: Sow 2 in. deep in April under glass for transplanting after danger of frost is past, or May–July in the open.

rows, 6 ft. between double rows.
CULTIVATION: Spray in dry weather to encourage setting. Pick regularly.
CROPPING: July–November.

Beet, Round or Globe
SEED: Sow 1 in. deep late March–July.
SPACING: 4 to 6 in. between plants, 12 in. between rows.
CULTIVATION: Best as an early crop for cooking when large enough.
CROPPING: June onwards.

Beet, Long-rooted
SEED: Sow $1\frac{1}{2}$ in. deep April–June.
SPACING: 6 to 8 in. between plants, 12 to 15 in. between rows.
CULTIVATION: Suitable for main crop and storing in sand when sufficiently mature.
CROPPING: July–March.

Broccoli (Sprouting and Cauliflower Heading and Calabrese)
SEED: Sow $\frac{1}{2}$ in. deep March–May. Transplant May–July.
SPACING: 24 in. between plants, 24 to 30 in. between rows.
CULTIVATION: Plant on firm soil. Draw earth up round stems and firm to prevent wind rocking in November.
CROPPING: October–May.

Brussels Sprouts
SEED: Sow $\frac{1}{2}$ in. deep in cold frames August–September, outdoors February–April. Transplant March–June.
SPACING: 24 to 30 in. between plants, 30 to 36 in. between rows.
CULTIVATION: Plant deeply to first pair of leaves in firm, rich soil. Stake large plants.
CROPPING: Pick as buttons October–March.

Cabbage (Summer)
SEED: Sow $\frac{1}{2}$ in. deep in frame in February, outdoors in March. Transplant in April.
SPACING: 18 to 24 in. between plants, 24 in. between rows.
CULTIVATION: Grow quick-maturing varieties.
CROPPING: June–August.

Cabbage (Autumn)
SEED: Sow $\frac{1}{2}$ in. deep in April. Transplant in May.
SPACING: 18 to 24 in. between plants, 24 in. between rows.
CULTIVATION: Choose hardy kind to withstand winter.
CROPPING: September–March.

Cabbage (Spring)
SEED: Sow $\frac{1}{2}$ in. deep mid-July to early August. Transplant September to early October.
SPACING: 12 to 14 in. between plants, 12 to 24 in. between rows.
CULTIVATION: Alternate plants can be used as early greens. Beware of fly, club root and caterpillars.
CROPPING: April–June.

Carrot
SEED: Sow $\frac{3}{4}$ to 1 in. deep in frame in February, outdoors March–July, covering seed lightly. Thin while small.
SPACING: 4 to 9 in. between plants, 9 to 12 in. between rows.
CULTIVATION: Plant in light soil: fresh manure encourages forking. Make successional sowings. Watch carrot fly.
CROPPING: June–April.

Cauliflower
SEED: Sow $\frac{1}{2}$ in. deep in frame September–October or February, outdoors March–May. Transplant March–April, or May–July.
SPACING: 24 in. between plants, 24 in. between rows.
CULTIVATION: Avoid checks in growth. Draw leaves over the curds to protect late batches.
CROPPING: May–November.

Celery
SEED: Sow $\frac{1}{4}$ in. deep under glass March–April. Transplant May–June.
SPACING: 12 in. between plants for a single row, 9 in. for a double row, 48 in. between rows.
CULTIVATION: Likes heavily manured soil. Water in when planting and dust with naphthalene against fly. Blanch by drawing earth up round stems, first protecting them with a paper collar. Protect from frost.
CROPPING: October–February.

Celery, Self-blanching
SEED: Sow $\frac{1}{4}$ in. deep under glass in March–April. Transplant May–June.
SPACING: 8 to 9 in. between plants, 8 to 9 in. between rows.
CULTIVATION: If planted in a square the leaves will cast sufficient shade to blanch without earthing up.
CROPPING: August–September.

Cress

SEED: Sow on the surface under glass September–April, outdoors April–September.

SPACING: Sow broadcast.

CULTIVATION: Takes three days longer to mature than mustard.

CROPPING: Any time.

Cucumber, Frame

SEED: Sow $\frac{1}{2}$ in. deep under glass January–May. Transplant February–June.

SPACING: 30 to 36 in. between plants.

CULTIVATION: It is important never to let the plants dry out. Remove male flowers to prevent pollination which will make fruits bitter.

CROPPING: March–October.

Cucumber, Ridge

SEED: Sow 1 in. deep under glass in mid-April, outdoors in May. Transplant May–June.

SPACING: 24 in. between plants, 48 in. between rows.

CULTIVATION: Suitable for gardener without glass. Nip out the tip when seven leaves have formed. It is not necessary to remove male flowers.

CROPPING: August–October.

Leeks

SEED: Sow $\frac{1}{2}$ in. deep in a frame in February, outdoors March–April. Transplant April–May.

SPACING: 8 to 10 in. between plants, 12 to 15 in. between rows.

CULTIVATION: Very hardy and one of the best winter vegetables. Requires a sunny site and generous manure in winter. Plant with a dibber.

CROPPING: September–May.

Lettuce

SEED: Sow $\frac{1}{2}$ in. deep under glass January–March and September–October, outdoors March–August and winter-hardy varieties in September.

SPACING: 8 to 10 in. between plants, 12 in. between rows.

CULTIVATION: Most of us sow too generously, resulting in a glut. Better to make small sowings, successively, once a fortnight. Dressings of manure or compost will reduce bolting. Cos lettuces require tying in. Seedlings transplant unwillingly, often only to bolt. September winter-hardy varieties are useful for the gardener without glass.

CROPPING: March onwards; January onwards; May–October; April–May.

Mustard

SEED: Sow on the surface under glass September–April, outdoors April–September.

SPACING: Sow broadcast.

CULTIVATION: Matures more quickly than cress; should be sown three days later.

CROPPING: Cut in leaf stage two to three weeks after sowing.

Onions

SEED: Sow $\frac{1}{2}$ in. deep February–March and August. Transplant April–May and March. Plant sets in March or April.

SPACING: 6 to 9 in. between plants, 12 in. between rows.

CULTIVATION: Protect onion sets from birds until rooted. Onions demand a deeply dug, heavily manured sunny site and fine soil texture.

CROPPING: August onwards; July onwards.

Onions, Salad

SEED: Sow $\frac{1}{2}$ in. deep at intervals during February–August.

SPACING: $\frac{1}{2}$ to 1 in. between plants, 9 to 12 in. between rows.

CULTIVATION: As for main crop.

CROPPING: Pull when young.

Parsley

SEED: Sow $\frac{1}{2}$ in. deep March–July.

Spacing: 6 in. between plants, 12 in. between rows.

CULTIVATION: Sow on well-drained, sunny ground near a path.

CROPPING: All the year round.

Parsnip

SEED: Sow $\frac{3}{4}$ in. deep March–May.

SPACING: 10 to 12 in. between plants, 12 to 15 in. between rows.

CULTIVATION: Avoid fresh manure, which encourages forking.

CROPPING: November–March. Can be left in ground and lifted when required.

Peas

SEED: Sow 2 in. deep in shelter or under cloches November–April for round-seeded varieties; main sowings of wrinkled peas from April onwards.

SPACING: Approximately 4 in. between plants, 18 to 60 in. between rows, depending on height of variety.

CULTIVATION: Mulch with manure during the summer.

CROPPING: June–October.

Potatoes

PLANT: March–May.

SPACING: 10 to 15 in. between plants, 20 to 28 in. between rows.

CULTIVATION: Grow earlies in a sheltered position, preferably a south border. Choose day for planting when tilth is just right. Spray with Bordeaux mixture against blight.

CROPPING: June onwards.

Rhubarb

PLANT: Strong crowns March–April.

SPACING: 18 to 30 in. between plants, 24 to 36 in. between rows.

CULTIVATION: Topdress with manure in February. Never let your plants waste their energy in flowering. Cover with pots or boxes for early use.

CROPPING: April–September.

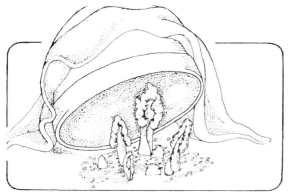

Forcing rhubarb under an upturned flower pot

Radishes, Summer

SEED: Sow $\frac{1}{2}$ in. deep February–September.
SPACING: 1 to 2 in. between plants, 6 in. between rows, or broadcast.
CULTIVATION: Rich soil preferred; must not suffer drought.
CROPPING: April–October.

Radishes, Winter

SEED: Sow $\frac{1}{2}$ in. deep end of July–August.
SPACING: 5 to 7 in. between plants, 12 in. between rows, or broadcast.
CROPPING: October–March.

Savoy

SEED: Sow $\frac{1}{2}$ in. deep March–May. Transplant April–June.
SPACING: 24 in. between plants, 24 to 30 in. between rows.
CULTIVATION: Very hardy: a useful crop for the northern gardener. January King is a grand variety.
CROPPING: October–March.

Shallots

PLANT: Sets 2 in. deep February–March.
SPACING: 8 in. between plants, 12 in. between rows.
CULTIVATION: An alternative crop to onions. Has no liking for fresh manure. Soil should be removed from around the bulbs in June to assist ripening.
CROPPING: July–February.

Spinach, Winter

SEED: Sow 1 in. deep July–August.
SPACING: 6 in. between plants, 12 in. between rows.

Removing unwanted side shoots in the leaf axils of tomatoes

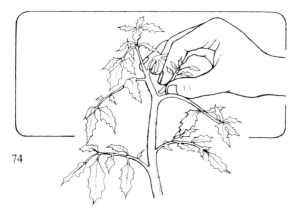

CULTIVATION: Winter spinach or Prickly Seeded are cultivated for their leaves. Water well and frequently to prevent plants running to seed.
CROPPING: March–May.

Spinach, Summer

SEED: Sow 1 in. deep February–May.
SPACING: 6 in. between plants, 12 in. between rows.
CULTIVATION: Water well in dry weather. A useful catch crop.
CROPPING: May–October.

Spinach Beet

SEED: Sow 1 in. deep April–August.
SPACING: 9 in. between plants, 12 to 15 in. between rows.
CULTIVATION: Useful in a drought, it is also known as perpetual spinach.
CROPPING: July–April.

Swede

SEED: Sow $\frac{1}{2}$ in. deep May–June.
SPACING: 9 in. between plants, 12 to 18 in. between rows.
CULTIVATION: A winter standby that grows better in the North and West than in the South East. Only succeeds in moist soils.
CROPPING: October–March.

Tomatoes

SEED: Sow $\frac{1}{2}$ in. deep January–February to grow under glass, March for outdoors. Transplant March–April indoors, end of May–June for outdoor varieties.
SPACING: 18 to 24 in. between plants, 30 in. between rows; 24 in. between plants, 36 to 40 in. between rows for outdoor varieties.
CULTIVATION: For raising outdoors, a rich soil is required in a sunny, sheltered position. Soil must be in good heart.
CROPPING: June–October; August–November.

Turnip

SEED: Sow $\frac{1}{2}$ in. deep March–July for summer crops; August–September for winter and storing.
SPACING: 6 to 9 in. between plants, 12 in. between rows.
CULTIVATION: Choose hardy varieties that will stand the winter.
CROPPING: May onwards; October onwards. Use when young, small and tender.

Vegetable Marrow

SEED: Sow 1 in. deep under glass in April; outdoors in May. Transplant at the end of May.
SPACING: 36 in. between plants for bush varieties, 48 in. for trailing; 36 to 48 in. between rows for bush varieties, 60 to 72 in. for trailing.
CULTIVATION: Enjoys a rich loam with a taste of well-rotted manure. Trailing plants should be pinched back: bush marrows do not require thinning or pinching and are suitable for small gardens.

Fruit

Few gardeners can afford to devote much land to fruit growing but the space afforded should be kept exclusively for fruit, except in the case of espalier-trained trees which can be grown against fences or walls in the flower garden. These take little space and will be found extremely decorative.

Fruit of the same kind should be blocked together in order to simplify feeding, netting or caging against birds. An open, well-drained situation, sheltered from the east wind should be chosen for this garden. Any dip or valley vulnerable to frost and deep shade is to be avoided.

The gardener will have to decide what proportion of the garden he means to devote to growing soft fruits–gooseberries, raspberries, currants and strawberries–and how much to tree fruits–apples, pears, plums, quince, peaches and cherries.

In very small gardens cordon or dwarf pyramids of apples and pears which have been grafted on dwarfing rootstock with especially slow-growing root systems are advised. But a large, free-growing pear on the lawn or at some focal point makes a fine specimen tree and is a star turn in the spring.

Fruit trees and certified soft fruit should be bought from a reputable nursery inspected by the Ministry of Agriculture. The nursery should be told the size of the garden, the nature of the soil, and if possible, the fruits and varieties that do well in the locality.

Planting

A well-drained medium loam suits most fruit. In the case of heavy soil the subsoil should be broken up. Chalk, gravel and dry, light soil will require additions of organic manure without making the mixture over-rich.

The importance of good drainage cannot be overstressed.

In general, planting is best done in the first week of November, though container-grown plants can be put in at any time provided conditions are suitable. Firm but rather shallow planting, no lower than the soil mark on the stem, is the rule.

Cultivation details are dealt with under the heading for individual fruits.

LIST OF FRUITS

Strawberry

Of all the soft fruits, the strawberry gives the fastest return.
SOIL: Rich, moisture-retentive soil, dressed with potash.
PLANTING: July–August. 15 in. between plants; 30 in. between rows.
FEEDING: Topdress with manure in autumn.
CULTIVATION: Remove blossoms during the first year to prevent fruiting. Plants about to fruit should be bedded with straw or black polythene to keep the crop clear of the soil. This should be removed after plants have fruited.
PROPAGATION: Strawberries lose vigour after three years. Healthy runners can be pegged down and rooted in small pots close to the parent plant in early July and severed in August. Remove unwanted runners promptly.
PICKING: Pick when the fruit is dry, being careful to include the calyx–the green sepals at the top where the stalk enters the fruit.
SPRAYING: In April, spray with malathion against greenfly.
VARIETIES: Royal Sovereign, has no rival, but is prone to virus disease. Cambridge Favourite, a heavy cropper but with a disappointing flavour. Grandi, a newcomer with the largest fruit; favourable flavour. Sans Rivale, perpetual fruiting, September; fair flavour, enjoys light soils. Alpine and Baron Solemacher, delicious small fruit, similar to the wild strawberry. Propagation by division.

Raspberry

This is the best soft fruit for the amateur. It is a quick, July cropper yielding a pound of fruit per foot.
SOIL: Likes a rich soil with high potash content. Seldom succeeds on chalk.
PLANTING: Autumn to spring. Shallow planting covering roots with 3 in. of soil. 18 to 24 in. apart; rows 6 ft. apart.
PRUNING: Cut down autumn and winter-planted canes to 6 to 12 in. from the ground in February. In subsequent years cut down old canes and burn them; train in five or six young suckers. Trim back tips of canes and tie in to wire supports stretched to posts 4 to 5 ft. high.
FEEDING: A taste of bonemeal in autumn, a March dressing of sulphate of potash at $\frac{3}{4}$ oz. per square yard, and a mulch in April with rotted manure are all welcome.
CULTIVATION: Water generously.
PROPAGATION: Stock is easily increased by suckers but new certified plants are advised.
SPRAYING: Beware the raspberry beetle, a wretched pest hatching out in May. It is best controlled by spraying or dusting with derris, in June, just before the fruit begins to colour.
VARIETIES: Lloyd George, medium sized; one of the best

Pegging down strawberry runners to form new plants

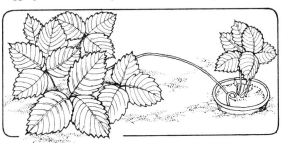

flavoured raspberries; a heavy cropper when healthy but vulnerable to virus disease. Malling Enterprise, large fruits; good flavour. September, a desirable autumn variety.

Black Currant

This is a fruit particularly high in vitamin C content.

SOIL AND POSITION: A sunny position preferred but will tolerate light shade. Gross feeder.

PLANTING: October or March. Spacing 5 ft. apart; 6 ft. between rows.

PRUNING: Cut back after planting to a bud 2 in. from ground. Do not allow fruiting in the first year. In subsequent years cut out weak growth to soil level after fruiting. Old plants benefit by being cut down to within 8 in. of the ground.

FEEDING: Dress with Nitro-chalk in March, 1 oz. to the square yard; phosphate dressings are also helpful. Moderate feeds of cow and poultry manure are appreciated.

CULTIVATION: Beware of damaging surface roots when hoeing.

PROPAGATION: Take 8-in. cuttings of current year's growth and place in sandy soil in autumn. Cut off close to a bud without removing any of the basal buds.

SPRAYING: Reversion is a prevalent virus disease of black currants. The symptoms are smaller but longer leaves, hairless buds and flowers failing to set fruit. Incurable; the plants are best burned. Big bud is a condition resulting in abnormally swollen buds due to gall-mite. Winter spray with tar oil, or lime sulphur wash as soon as the leaves begin to form in spring (grape stage).

VARIETIES: Early: Boskoop Giant, fine flavour. Laxton's Giant, largest fruit; sweet and juicy. Mid-season: Seabrook's Black, heavy cropper, fair flavour. Late: Amos Black, good flavour.

Red and White Currant

The white currant requires the same treatment as the red.

SOIL: Prefers light to rich. An ounce of sulphate of potash to a square yard should be worked in when preparing the ground.

PLANTING: October–March, the earlier the better. Space the bushes 5 ft. apart; 6 ft. between rows.

PRUNING: Cut back branches halfway to outward pointing buds and the side shoots to two buds from their base. Later, as the plants age, older branches may be cut back hard and replaced by new growth.

FEEDING: As for black currant.

PROPAGATION: By cuttings as for black currant. Lower buds should be removed to obtain a bush with a leg or main stem.

SPRAYING: Against aphids.

VARIETIES: Early: Earliest of Fourlands, long bunches, heavy cropper; the best all-round red currant. Mid-season: Laxton's No. 1, good sized fruit very freely produced. Late: Wilson's Long Bunch, medium-sized fruit; regular cropper. White currants: White Versailles, strong grower, large, sweet berry.

Gooseberry

SOIL AND SITUATION: Happy in well-drained deep loam with plenty of humus. Heavy soil should be cultivated and lightened with peat, straw and grit. Requires regular additions of potash. Open site protected from north and east winds.

PLANTING: Autumn or winter. 5 to 6 ft. apart. Deep planting should be avoided.

PRUNING: In winter prune back shoots of two- or three-year-old plants halfway to a bud. Cut back lateral growths to 3 in. and cut out weak wood. Old plants can be more severely treated and the leading shoots cut back harder. Keep the centre of the bushes open by thinning the main branches. Summer: from the third week in June reduce lateral growths to 5 leaves.

FEEDING: Winter dressing of manure desirable. Early spring feed of sulphate of potash, $\frac{3}{4}$ to $1\frac{1}{2}$ oz. per square yard, is necessary to counteract any potash deficiency.

CULTIVATION: Beware when hoeing or forking not to damage surface roots.

PROPAGATION: As for currants. Be sure to remove lower buds.

PICKING: Fruit is best thinned. Small berries are useful for tarts.

SPRAYING: American mildew is controlled by spraying with lime sulphur or a modern systemic fungicide such as Benlate. Varieties which are sulphur shy, such as Leveller, can be sprayed with a solution of $\frac{1}{2}$ lb. soft soap and 2 lb. of washing soda in 10 gallons of water. Sawfly caterpillar should be sprayed with derris immediately it is sighted. There are often two or three broods of this pest in a season.

VARIETIES: Early: Keepsake, pale green; excellent flavour. Mid-season: Golden Drop, yellow, small berries with a good flavour. Late: White Lion, very good flavour. Leveller, one of the largest; greenish-yellow berries produced in quantity.

Other Berries

Large blackberries, superior to their hedgerow brothers, are easily grown. A single plant will supply an abundance of fruit but requires 15 to 20 ft. of space against a fence or wiring.

Bedford Giant is the earliest and largest; Himalayan Giant presents huge trusses and crops, and Oregon Evergreen is blessed by being thornless.

The Loganberry is a hybrid berry and will grow almost anywhere. There is also a thornless variety. Good for cooking and excellent for bottling. All fruit must be picked when dry.

The Blueberry, Boysenberry, Japanese Wineberry, and the red-fruited Cranberry are willing growers but are not to everybody's tastes.

Apple

Apples are the most widely grown of all fruits. The trained pyramid or cordon (restricted to a single stem), and dwarf or semi-dwarf bush forms suit the small garden, taking up least space and simplifying spraying, pruning and picking.

Some varieties are self-fertile; others require a suitable pollinator, and there are those that need a third pollinator to fruit satisfactorily. Nurserymen are ready to advise on suitable mating. Trees often fail to bear fruit due to lack of suitable pollinators and it is unwise to plant a single tree unless there are other apples in the neighbourhood.

PLANTING: November–March. Dwarf pyramids, 5 ft. apart; bushes and pyramids, 12 ft.; cordons, 2 ft.

PRUNING: Warning–the harder a tree is pruned the more exuberant the growth. Prune young trees lightly to encourage fruiting, cut back old trees to encourage new growth. Pruning is important; young trees, if left unpruned, will fruit early but lose vigour later and may resort to fruiting every other year only.

Apples fruit on two-year-old or older wood. The tree's framework is built up during the first four years. Pruning is carried out according to the tree's habit of growth–whether it is a tip-bearer, such as Bramley's Seedling or Worcester Permain or a spur-bearer, such as James Grieve and Cox's Orange Pippin. A fair number of shoots must be left on tip-bearers or the crop will suffer.

Summer pruning: July and early August. Shorten shoots to four leaves or so, according to vigour.

Winter pruning: November. Reduce side shoots to within two buds or nine for tip-bearers from the main stem. Shorten leading shoots to about 10 in. of the new growth or a third of their growth. Once trained, little attention is needed apart from removing crossing, unwanted or unhealthy branches.

Root pruning and bark ringing are methods of curbing an over-vigorous tree which fails to fruit, but this is work for an experienced gardener.

FEEDING: First year, spring manure dressing. Second year onwards, dressings of 1 oz. of sulphate of ammonia and $\frac{1}{2}$ oz. sulphate of potash to the square yard. Every two or three years superphosphate, $1\frac{1}{2}$ to 2 oz. to the square yard.

CULTIVATION: Trees making too much growth can be checked by grassing down, sowing beneath the trees a mixture of Wild White Clover and rye grass, and keeping this short.

PROPAGATION: By budding in July, or grafting in March or April. Not advised for the beginner.

THINNING: On occasion it is necessary to thin the crop, allowing only two fruits on one spur. King fruit–that is the apple at the centre of the cluster–must be removed when the size of a walnut. Thin after nature's June drop.

PICKING: The pips are brown when ripe. Fruit when given the slightest twist should come away if ripe.

STORING: Store in a cool, damp atmosphere. Wrap the fruit in polythene bags or newspaper when storage conditions are inadequate. Do not seal the wrapping or make it airtight, particularly in the case of polythene bags, as a little ventilation is necessary.

SPRAYING: Winter: A tar-oil wash, once every two years when the trees are dormant, will destroy aphids (greenfly) and other eggs.

April: BHC spray at bud burst to green cluster stage (perhaps the most important spray of all) will control caterpillars, winter moth, aphids, apple capsid, apple sucker and scale insects.

April: Captan spray at pink bud stage, against scab.

May: BHC spray at petal fall against apple sawfly.

June: BHC against codling moth.

Mid-June: Chlorbenzilate, or a similar summer ovicide, against red spider mite.

Prompt action with a suitable spray and correct timing is the secret of success. Once the enemy is established it is difficult to dislodge. Fruit should not be sprayed when in flower. The insecticide may kill bees and other pollinating insects.

All diseased fruit should be picked up and burned.

OTHER PROBLEMS: Canker: The affected branch should be cut away to sound wood and the wound treated with Stockholm tar or other wound dressing compound. Mildew: Use lime sulphur or Benlate spray or dinocap for the sulphur-shy.

VARIETIES: Dessert varieties: July–August, Scarlet Pimpernel, red; crisp; early. September–October, James Grieve; soft, juicy fruit with a good flavour; frost resistant. October–December, Egremont Russet; yellow fruit, first-rate flavour. November–December, Sunset; rather like Cox but sweeter and easier to grow. December–January, Cox's Orange Pippin; temperamental, good in the South of England; delicious flavour.

Cooking Varieties: July–August, Early Victoria; good, cooks to a froth. November–February, Howgate Wonder; regular cropper, a better size for the small garden than Bramley. Crawley Beauty; self-fertile, good flavour.

Pear

Trees grown on quince rootstocks are best suited to the small garden. Some varieties, such as Williams', are not compatible with quince and these are double worked (a compatible variety being used as an intermediate stock.) Pears are not quite so hardy as apples.

SOIL: Good soil, sunny position. A sheltered position is desirable–near a south or south-west wall is ideal. Fruit can be netted against frost in cold areas.

PLANTING: Plant between November and March, making sure that the union mark on the stem is at least 4 in. above soil level, and mulch with manure. Space cordon and dwarf pyramids 3 to 4 ft. apart; bush, 15 ft. apart.

PRUNING: Much the same as for apples (see above) but slightly lighter when young; more severely on older trees, cutting back leaders, shortening side shoots and removing unwanted spurs.

FEEDING: As for apples (see above), but Doyenné du Comice and choosy varieties require a rich diet.

PROPAGATION: By grafting in March, budding in July–August.

PICKING: Pick when the fruit comes away with the slightest twist. It is better to pick too early rather than too late.

STORING: The best method is to lay out the fruit singly, not wrapped, on shelves in the dark. A temperature of 5 to 10°C. (40 to 50°F.) is ideal. Regular inspection of the fruit in store is essential. Bring the pears into the living room for 24 hours before eating.

SPRAYING: As for apples (see p. 77). Beware of scab.

VARIETIES: September: Williams' Bon Crétien; English, good flavour. Merton Pride; a newcomer with juicy fruit. October–November: Conference; the easiest to grow, hardy and reliable. November: Doyenné du Comice; a pear *par excellence* for most of us; warm districts only and a south wall. December–April: Catillac; large fruit, the best cooker.

Cherry (Sweet)

Sweet cherries are too large for small gardens; there is no dwarfing root stock. These large trees are difficult to crop and protect from birds. Fan training is advised on west or south-west walls, but even this may not be completely satisfactory. They are slow to fruit and require pollinators.

SOIL: Light loam with a lime content, sunny position.

PLANT: November to March, 25 ft. apart; 15 to 18 ft. for fan-trained trees.

PRUNING: Avoid winter pruning for fear of silver-leaf disease. Remove crossing and diseased wood only in March.

FEEDING: Mulch with manure in late spring. Give an occasional dressing of sulphate of potash at 1 to $1\frac{1}{2}$ oz. to the sq. yd. Every two or three years dress with super-phosphate at 2 to 3 oz. per sq. yd.

SPRAYING: Spray, if necessary, with malathion before bud-burst stage against cherry fruit moth caterpillars.

VARIETIES: June: Early Rivers, black. Mid-late July: Bigarreau Napoleon, white.

Cherry (Sour Cooking)

PLANTING: 15 to 20 ft. apart, can be fan trained on 9- to 10-ft. high walls.

CULTURE: As for sweet cherry.

VARIETIES: August–September: Morello; good flavour, happy in a semi-shade position, self-fertile. Cut fruit with scissors. July: Kentish Red; self-fertile.

Peach

The majority of varieties are self-fertile but hand pollination with a camel-hair brush is helpful.

SOIL: Good ordinary soil with a taste of lime and a sprinkling of bonemeal. Efficient drainage is essential. Peaches grow best trained against a south-facing wall.

PLANTING: October to early November, spaced 15 to 24 ft. apart.

PRUNING: After fruiting or in November replace the old fruiting stems by training in new growth. Maintaining an even spacing of the branches is important.

FEEDING: Mulch generously with manure in spring or early summer. An occasional sprinkling of Nitro-chalk is helpful.

THINNING: Young plants must not be allowed to fruit in the first year or at any time to overcrop. Thin to leave single fruit at approximately 9-in. intervals. The thinning is carried out twice when the fruits are the size of marbles and walnuts.

PROTECTION: The fruit requires protection from birds. Repaired fishnets (if old curtains are not available) are the cheapest way of providing protection.

VARIETIES: Mid-August: Peregrine; brightly coloured fruit with white flesh and a good flavour; most reliable.

Plum

Plums include gages and damsons.

All are early flowering and vulnerable to spring frosts and grow well against a warm wall. The gardener should ask the nurseryman's advice on the choice of rootstock. Plums do not grow well as cordons or espaliers. Some plums are self-fertile but others need a suitable pollinator. (The nuseryman or the R.H.S. will advise on this.)

SOIL: Heavy loam and a fully sunny position.

PLANTING: Plant firmly and stake standards. Space common plum 12 to 15 ft. apart, fan-trained trees 15 to 18 ft.

PRUNING: Leave unpruned the first year, then prune as for apples but not before the end of March to avoid silver-leaf disease which often enters through wounds made in winter. June and July are the best months for pruning.

FEEDING: As for apples (see p. 77).

SPRAYING: Liquid malathion against aphids in spring and summer.

GUMMING: Gum sometimes exudes from the fruit. This is a physiological condition possibly due to changeable weather; it is not a disease. There is no very satisfactory control for this trouble but an application of Bordeaux mixture just before leaf fall may prove helpful.

VARIETIES: Mid-August: Denniston's Superb Gage; yellow, good flavour, hardy and dependable. Early Transparent Gage; apricot-yellow fruit with a lovely flavour. Mid-September: Kirke's; large dark purple fruits of excellent flavour, a little temperamental. September–October: Coe's Golden Drop; pale yellow, very sweet and my favourite; superb when gathered warm from a wall.

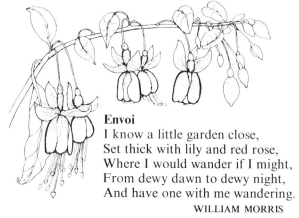

Envoi
I know a little garden close,
Set thick with lily and red rose,
Where I would wander if I might,
From dewy dawn to dewy night,
And have one with me wandering.
WILLIAM MORRIS

Index

Abbreviations:
d = line drawing
p = photograph